PENNY WISE

THE COMPLETE GUIDE TO SAVING MONEY WITH ONLINE PENNY AUCTIONS

KEN KNELLY
JOSHUA WALDRON

Visit the website at pennywisethebook.com for more information.

The publishers are not responsible for websites (or their content) not owned by the publishers.

Cover design by Studio JWAL LLC.

Icons are part of the DefaultIcon set by InteractiveMania.com.

First Edition: October 2011

ISBN: 0615521665
ISBN-13: 978-0-615-52166-4

CONTENTS

PREFACE

I stumbled across an advertisement promoting penny auctions in the summer of 2009. This new type of online buying offered name-brand gift cards for a few cents.

The skeptical part of me immediately dismissed the deals as another online scam, poised to dupe unsuspecting victims foolish enough to participate. But the curious side had to know how the business model worked.

I did some quick research before registering on a penny auction site for the first time. Media coverage and information of any kind on these auctions – online or otherwise – was virtually non-existent then.

This first site gave five free bids for registering. It didn't require any credit card information to join. I figured there was nothing to lose.

That same day, still suspicious, I participated in my first penny auction for a $15 gift card. Using three free bids, I won the auction for less than a dime.

The site directed me to a checkout page. I used PayPal to purchase the gift card without revealing any personal credit card information.

Even after paying, I figured there would be some catch.

Three days later, the gift card arrived in the mailbox.

From that point forward, I was in. Learning more about how this new online phenomenon worked, I discovered there were indeed pitfalls along the way if you weren't careful.

Shopping for bargains would never be the same.

By December 2009, I launched a website called Penny Auction List. This site was the first carefully filtered directory of penny auctions on the web. It featured penny auction tips, strategies, and news.

I started introducing family and friends to penny auctions, emphasizing the great deals waiting to be had. As time went on, I continued to score great deals, landing over $12,000 worth of items for about half the cost elsewhere online and far below the retail sticker price. Other careful bidders, I discovered, could do just as well and better.

Some items went to immediate use in the house. The rest were distributed as gifts for family, friends, and those in need.

Meanwhile, the penny auction landscape was changing. New sites opened and closed regularly, and many media outlets began covering penny auctions for the first time.

Most of the coverage featured unsuccessful bidders voicing complaints and frustration. Many concerns stemmed from a lack of understanding and wrong expectations, with others based on bad auction sites.

A book about penny auctions was desperately needed. Something simple and direct, useful and productive.

I enlisted Ken Knelly, a friend and former journalist, to co-author a definitive guide to penny auctions. He asked good questions, brought his own healthy dose of skepticism, and helped guide the thought, writing, and editing processes.

We sketched out chapters, crunched numbers, conducted interviews, emailed incessantly, and burned the midnight oil – all with the goal of producing the first comprehensive handbook for bidders. The goal is to help readers win more often, save more dollars, and avoid common mistakes.

We're proud of what we've done, and we hope you enjoy the book.

Joshua Waldron

1

PITCHING PENNIES

"If you would be wealthy, think of saving as well as getting."
—Founding Father Benjamin Franklin

It's a pretty good wager Heyyou, Whodat12, and Fanzienanzie have never met before. If they did, it might well have been in the lumber aisle at a neighborhood Lowe's.

On this workaday Tuesday, the trio is among a couple handfuls of devoted bidders aiming for a $100 Lowe's gift card. As the bidding soars past $13.56, the would-be shoppers are hot on the trail, each aiming for a bargain and paying for the privilege.

Watching the auction at a distance is like watching a horse race, except the horses in this race change and you have no idea when they'll hit the finish line. It keeps moving.

It ends a few minutes later with Nvartko – a late entry to the fray – the winner. For $16.43, plus $1.99 shipping, plus the cost of the penny bids – at 60 cents a pop – a card will soon be on its way.

If he (or she) threw 25 penny bids out there, and assuming Nvartko paid for all of them and didn't rely on ones obtained for free or gained as part of other auction wins, then the cost of a

$100 card arriving in the mailbox about a week later was a grand total of $33.42.

Not bad.

Some folks do a lot better at these mini-contests. Gift cards can sell for – and do – literally pennies plus shipping. Computers, games, and toys have all been scooped up at comparable, eye-popping bargains.

On the other side, some folks do worse. Some walk away with nothing but an adrenalin rush and a hangover-type letdown.

If any of Nvartko's competitors want to get that card and load up on plywood, they'll have to buy the Lowe's card at face value plus shipping. At some auctions, like this one that took place on Oklahoma City-based QuiBids, losing bidders can apply the value of the paid-for, 60-cent penny bids used in the rush to win toward their purchase. At others, the loss needs to be chalked up to experience.

Welcome to the world of penny auctions.

GETTING PENNY WISE

This book's foundation is built on the successful bidding experience of co-author Josh Waldron. After trials, errors, and a good bit of examination, Josh took home nearly $12,500 worth of items over a year and a half at a real, everything-factored-in net cost of a little more than $7,000.

That amounts to paying roughly 42 percent less than the price at discount places like Amazon.com. The savings were even higher if based on the manufacturer's suggested retail price on the label or quoted on penny auction sites themselves.

The success wasn't overnight and it wasn't on a few sites. It came through winning more than 330 auctions and participating on 44 different penny auction sites through August 2011.

His average net loss of just more than $42 on 21 of the sites was offset by an average net gain of nearly $264 on the other 23 sites. Over time he learned to curb his losses, recognizing site deficiencies like slow timers, and move on. He also learned how and when to keep bidding.

The Penny Auction List website that followed, as well as the research done for this book by both co-authors, yielded more lessons.

First, let's cut to the chase.

Are penny auctions worth it? Are they a rip-off? Do you need to keep reading?

The short answers are: They certainly can be; some are; and we hope so.

The longer answers, drawing on experience and countless conversations with penny auction owners and operators, go something like this:

Can you save money with penny auctions? Yes.

Will you get rich? No.

Can you sustain net winnings over time? Yes.

Will you win on all sites? No.

Can you do better than Josh? We'd like to think so. Some bidders we talked to in writing this book do.

Will you pick up big screen televisions for a few dimes? Possibly, but don't count on it. They are harder to land than other merchandise.

Is all of this worth your time? That depends.

If you like shopping online, hunting for a bargain, and doing both with a thrill of victory thrown in, then penny auctions can definitely deliver for you.

If you are only happy when you save hundreds of dollars at a time on big ticket items, are easily frustrated when you lose, and aren't in the mood for the gift cards and smaller merchandise within your grasp, then you're probably better off doing something else.

Look at it this way: Josh generated an extra $300 a month (or the net savings of more than $5,000 divided by 18 months) through a penny auction hobby. Josh operated on a limited budget, and penny auctions provided less-expensive gifts and savings on everything from shopping to gasoline.

That's a pretty good track record. For Josh, the deals are worth the effort.

If it sounds worthwhile to you, then keep reading. We'll aim to help you do as well or better.

If that sounds like too much time for too little gain, or even too much risk for too little gain, we get it. It's better for you to decide that up front than drive down the penny auction highway any farther.

We can say this with authority: You won't always win. Sometimes you will frustratingly lose. And some sites you pick off the beaten path may be poorly run or dishonest.

If you can consider that a cost of doing business, then read on.

PENNY AUCTION SCAM

We'll get into some of the history of penny auctions in a little bit. Before then, we'd like to hit on something you may be wondering about.

The "s" word.

Penny auctions, run well and above board, are a legitimate business model. We'll outline for you just how they work. Even so, there are sites that use shady tactics, fake bidding, rigged clocks, and more. They are scams.

💡 COMMON CENTS

Every area has its own unique terminology. "Strike,""ball," and "foul," for example, hardly make sense to someone who's never set foot on a diamond. (Yes, that kind of diamond, not the other kind.) The language of penny auctions isn't difficult, but it's important to know what certain words and phrases mean as you go. Look for Common Cents boxes through the book. They're helpful insights into terms, concepts, and applications that hang in and around the penny auction world.

Regulators – who have yet to really get into the game in all but a few states – have clamped the lid on some auctions. In

August 2011, the Federal Trade Commission issued a consumer alert describing the penny auction process and advising potential bidders to "recognize some of the pitfalls before you get caught in a bidding frenzy."

Some sites have collapsed under their own weight of bad marketing, poor quality, and lousy business decisions. Indeed, some we'll talk about have drawn literally millions of dollars in venture capital only to go belly-up.

It's also a fair question to ask whether the whole penny auction proposition is a losing one. Some academic studies focus on this challenge.

Ned Augenblick, a Stanford University economist, found "in aggregate, players significantly overbid" for auction items, leading to large profits for the penny auction business. Overall, he found, players generally collect small or negative winnings.

Augenblick concluded there are similarities to gambling, but there are also differences, such as the role of skill for winning players and "no obvious deception or manipulation" of the players.

Three economists from Brigham Young University found video game-related items in particular showed aggressive bidding and higher profits for auction sites. It also found penny auctions are "not any more lucrative than standard auction formats" for sellers. It also noted concerns about "shill bidding" that can be manipulated to generate more dollars for owners.

WHAT'S AHEAD

We've set the book up logically to help you understand what this new world is about.

If you want to pick and choose, here's a closer look at what's ahead:

Chapter 2 examines how we got here and gives you a picture of what this business is – from literally mom-and-pop to an emerging leader.

That's followed by a look inside the business model in Chapter 3. This can no-doubt be a money-making business, but it has not turned out to be the license to print money that a back-of-napkin analysis would lead you to believe. Some pretty big outfits have dumped big bucks into these online sales bins and lost. Turns out it is not so easy to succeed.

🏆 PENNY POINTS

These little break-out boxes aim to lay out a simple path to success on a given point or tactic we've explained more deeply in the text. It is critical to have a plan and an approach as you play penny auctions. Look for Penny Points boxes through the book. These helpful snapshots can help you see or apply lessons from the book in a direct way.

In Chapter 4, we turn to the basics. If you're new to penny auctions, you need to read this chapter. It covers the fundamentals and formats and will answer the up-front questions many newbies have.

Chapters 5 and 6 take it up a level. We'll walk through buying items, studying websites, strategies, and tips. In Chapter 7, we hit some more advanced issues. These are the types of things you'll need to know to be in a position to do better and not lose lots of pennies.

Later in the book, we take a few extra steps for the doctoral-level students among us.

Chapter 8 looks at what you can do with stuff you win and get in the mail. You may not want to keep it, after all. There are ways to do well here.

In Chapter 9, we delve into the realm of starting your own website. This is not for everyone, but it is something more than a few folks think about. We'll help you work through the issues and see more closely if this is worth pursuing on your end.

Finally, Chapter 10 is the Piggybank. We throw lots of links and some of our book sources at you. This can be a resource area of some good use, we hope.

Enjoy the rest of the book, and save up your pennies.

2

LAY OF THE LAND

"I didn't want to be greedy. It's a mark of bad character, and I always believed that pigs go the slaughterhouse."
—Publisher and philanthropist Walter Annenberg

Jeremy Hetrick got an idea.

"I was watching TV and saw an ad on a football game," he said. "'Get an iPod for 99 percent off.' I pulled it up on my laptop, bought a bid pack, and lost $30."

An idea was loosed, though. And BidPigs was born in February 2010.

Today, out of a house and garage in Pennsylvania, Hetrick and his wife average about three completed penny auctions a night, mostly gift cards. They're making a go of it, but not enough to quit a day job.

Reward points for frequent auction players, a fun website, T-shirts, and hats. Plus making sure buyers actually get what they win sent to them in the mail, something a run of renegade sites failed to do.

That's BidPigs' road to success.

Is it working?

BidPigs shipped north of $250,000 worth of products in its first year and change, Hetrick said. But the costs of goods sold, which for the most part he pays for in advance, are right at the heels of the revenue side.

'We're not getting killed too badly," he said. "We scratched some capital together, low investment. I still believe in the potential of it. If we had more money to throw into marketing ...."

Four months before Hetrick started his site, some young friends with University of Oklahoma connections took a run of their own.

And what a run it's been.

QuiBids (think "quick bids") launched with about a half-dozen people on board – most with an OU pedigree. They brought skills in marketing, computer programming, and analytics – the three keys to penny auction success.

Intrigued by now-failed pioneer Swoopo (more on them later), and determined to make a business model stick, the venture has done well by almost any measure.

With more than 115 employees and two floors of a 22-story Oklahoma City office building to their name – a space compared to a high energy game room, QuiBids is the market leader among penny auction sites in terms of revenues, auctions, and profits.

"You have to have economies of scale to make it work," said CEO Matt Beckham. "It's harder to get into the space now, harder for new sites to get credit card processing."

It may be tough, but QuiBids seems to be in a good spot.

Even so, the developing penny auction landscape is far from settled.

PAYING TO PLAY

Now a fundamental part of e-commerce, auctions trace their roots to several hundred years before Christ. They existed in ancient Greece, and the word "auction" itself derives from the Latin *auctio*, from the verb *augere*, meaning "to increase."

The role of auctions, however, was not central to exchanging goods on a large scale until the 18th century. In examining the more recent move to Internet auctions, *The Economist* magazine in 1999 reviewed the history of auctions, noting they were long limited to "agricultural and other commodity markets, fine art and antiques, and ... some types of financial securities."

Moving to a whole new world exploded with the Internet, which opened the number of buyers and sellers and the corresponding range of goods.

The biggest game-changer in this regard was eBay. Started in 1995 by a computer programmer, eBay posted net income of $1.8 billion on revenues of $9.2 billion in 2010. Its more than 17,000 employees work for a worldwide company that has spawned such household names as PayPal and StubHub.

Ten years after the launch of eBay came the beginnings of penny auctions.

The bidding-fee method – selling penny bids for a price, a pay to play approach, and an extended time clock – was hatched first in Germany and most successfully initially by Telebid, which became known as Swoopo in 2008.

The penny auctions that followed built on the eBay foundation of user connections and familiarity with paying online, mixing in the new frontier amplified by Swoopo.

The result fuses desired products with entertainment.

Whether they are "auctions" in the traditional sense is a subject of debate. Many say spending money to buy a right to bid is more like gambling.

 COMMON CENTS

Gambling

Webster's Dictionary defines gambling as "the act of playing for stakes in the hope of winning." We often associate gambling with games of chance, such as blackjack or roulette, and random-type activities, such as lotteries and bingo. There is little you can do beyond choosing a number or color in determining the outcome. In applying the definition to penny auctions, it depends to some extent on how you approach it as to whether it is gambling. You can control how you bid and have more than a hope, but there are elements you can't control that are similar to gambling.

"When people are bidding again and again and again and they don't actually win the item in the end, that's very much like gambling," Professor Mark Griffiths of Nottingham Trent University said in an interview with the BBC.

Auction companies, for the most part, say skill and tactics are involved.

Either way, technology and opportunity meet edge-of-your-seat battles for a bargain in penny auctions, with the buyer needing to be more careful than eBay players who risk no financial loss.

EXPLOSIVE GROWTH

How much of a business have penny auctions become? Hard figures for sales, profits, and websites are difficult to nail down, but tracking of transactions and interviews with principals at a range of auction sites pegs U.S. sales at more than $500 million in 2010.

Today, hundreds of websites offer the format, and countless sites exist to track, critique, and promote bidding – some owned or controlled by the sellers themselves.

An estimated 100 sites launched in the U.S. after Swoopo advanced in 2008. Interest ballooned after that, with many start-ups looking at penny auctions as a license to print money.

If an iPad sells for $20, and bids are 60 cents each, the seller grosses $1,200 for a device they can buy for a fraction of the price.

Do the math and you can come up with better deals.

The momentum of growth, though, has stalled a bit, with many dozens of sites now insolvent. Major players like QuiBids, along with other larger sites like Beezid, SkoreIt!, and BidRivals, are separating themselves. Smaller operators, without the economies of scale, are finding the road ahead difficult and not as easy as anticipated.

Joe Crivello, the Chief Operating Officer at SkoreIt!, a Wisconsin-based site launched in 2010, has never seen a more complex business model.

"We did 12 months of due diligence," said Crivello, noting the SkoreIt! team's experience in sectors like retail, real estate, and energy. "The number of new entrants per month is decelerating. We anticipate there will be less than 10 major operators within a few years."

Indeed, the landscape is littered with start-ups gone bad – including Swoopo itself.

In early 2011, Swoopo's parent, Munich-based Entertainment Shopping AG, filed for bankruptcy protection. Along with the fall, items went undelivered to winning bidders.

Observers say Swoopo's sharp growth was both its greatest strength and its greatest weakness. Operations in seven nations at one time got it attention and buyers. But the business burned through its capital like a pyro on the Fourth of July, bought licenses for software it wouldn't need, and was not nearly as good at marketing as at technology.

And when it comes to growing a penny auction site, marketing is king.

OPPORTUNITIES AHEAD

In some ways, penny auction sites sit at the frontier of a perfect storm.

As the economy struggles to recover, and some wonder whether the U.S. itself sits on the threshold of its own lost decade of growth in the midst of burgeoning national debt and a flat job market, the idea of buying still-coveted tech devices and gift cards at a bargain is a built-in advantage.

Consumers are hurting. Having drained their savings and seen their home equity vaporize, buyers have cut spending. A recent report by the Federal Reserve Bank of San Francisco said consumption per person fell about $7,300, or about $175 per person per month, from December 2007 to May 2011.

The implications are huge.

Tax rebates, tax holidays, Social Security payroll tax cuts, and more have been tried to boost the long-standing two-thirds of the economy that stands on consumer spending. Anything to jack up the sputtering machine.

With such a backdrop, the strengths for penny auctions can be anchored on one side by the economy and bargain-hunting. People looking to save money in places they are already finding deals – online – can move in the direction of penny auctions, if the sites are attractive and stable enough.

 COMMON CENTS

Penny

There were more than 2.8 billion pennies in circulation in 2011, a total that makes up roughly 58 percent of all domestic coins, according to the U.S. Mint. That's a pretty penny. Of course, in penny auction land, it's less about pennies than what they cost. And in penny auctions, they cost more than, well, a penny. In an online auction, bids rise in increments of one cent each. Every time you bid, the cost of the item goes up that much. When it's over, winners pay the cost of the item. The cost of your actual penny bids, though, are typically 60 cents each.

To boost such prospects, three online penny auction companies formed a trade association to create a sustainable model for protecting consumers and promoting legitimate options for penny auction sales. The Entertainment Auction Association was developed in late 2010 by BidCactus, the now-defunct Swoopo, and BigDeal, which was taken over by BidCactus in August 2011.

Its impact on the industry so far, limited at best, is less important than what the drive to put it together says: Stability is at the root of hoped-for success.

On the other side, the major players see entertainment, buzz, and – to the extent they can create it – fun added to the economic roots of future growth.

Penny auctions are increasingly positioning themselves as a place to play in a sandbox, mixing in deals and focusing on marketing to get the story told.

Think FarmVille on Facebook meets a new kind of farmer's market online, a fact we'll delve into more with Chapter 3.

CHALLENGES AHEAD, TOO

Even as penny auctions are positioned for success, there are clouds. The challenges are on a range of fronts – customer retention, gambling aspects, regulation, and credibility. Any one of these stand to stunt the growth of penny auctions and some have the potential to cripple it if handled poorly by the industry.

 **PENNY POINTS**

Entertainment Auction Association (EAA)
The EAA was envisioned as an industry trade group. Its impact remains to be seen, but its stated code of conduct is a good launching point for sound practices.

1. Real name, email, and address will be prominently displayed.
2. No employees, shill bidders, or bots bidding on the site.
3. Ship all items as promised at the shipping and handling cost displayed.
4. Have a clear refund policy for unused bids and abide by that policy.
5. Do not create fake testimonials, fake quotes, or fake promotional material.
6. Comply with the FTC's truth-in-advertising policies.
7. Do not make any fraudulent claims in advertising or on website.

On the retention side, auctions need to keep the players they have on their websites. Many academics say penny auctions are a losing proposition and, as we'll explore further in the book, it can be easier to win auctions in the beginning than it is later, particularly if you lack a strategy.

For those who equate penny auctions to gambling, the comparison to Las Vegas is apt. Planes arrive daily in Sin City, carrying loads of ready-made losers as cargo. When they fall on the bad side of the percentages and head back home, casinos pocket their money and the gamblers take home the memories.

Penny auction sites can't rely on the same model, even if they don't look at themselves as gambling in the same way. They need new players even as they keep from grinding up old ones.

The "buy-it-now" feature on many auction sites is one way to keep customers. The fall-back option, which we'll discuss more in Chapter 4, can be a drain on the bottom line of sites and is another reason why the future is likely to have fewer auction companies with larger economies of scale.

Also on the horizon, perhaps, is a greater role for government regulation.

Class action lawsuits in multiple jurisdictions, attorneys general and regulators in some states, and the recent federal crackdown on online poker sites, all portend increased scrutiny for those penny auction sites remaining in the game.

The suits and scrutiny stem from out-of-business websites that left customers without merchandise, in-business sites that break the law, and calls from some consumer activists who say penny auctions are like horse racing without the betting windows.

Whether penny auctions are actually gambling is an open question. Certainly the adrenalin-like rush of having an Apple in your eye can keep you hitting the bid button beyond the appropriate time. Some operators, though, say the business model is not much different from a high-end auction house that charges bidders a paddle fee to participate whether they win or not.

"A bid is a deterministic action, not a random act," said Joe Crivello, of SkoreIt!. "The only people determining the winner are the people who make the bids. People stop bidding because they feel further participation would not be positive, not because somebody took away their opportunity."

Larger sites say they are not opposed to government regulation entirely and don't see it as a deal-breaker for their businesses, even as some early steps by a few states and the FTC have fined or closed sites. The badge of meeting regulatory standards could push out bad players and boost their own credibility, they say.

Credibility is a focus, particularly with the high-profile exit of Swoopo. It was enough to prompt QuiBids in August 2011 to pay accounting giant Grant Thornton to examine its operation. The firm verified its bids are placed by "bona fide users," bidding is not manipulated to "inflate the bid price or affect who wins," and its orders are shipped.

"Everybody is sensationalizing cases of people getting ripped off," said Jeremy Hetrick, of BidPigs. "A lot of blame is on the door of penny auctions collectively, with advertising and marketing. If I tell you you can get a product at 99 percent off, that's what you expect. You can't make it look like it's a guarantee."

UPWARD MOBILITY

Some would-be penny auction businesses think they see the future, and it's a mobile one, with "gold in them thar hills."

California-based Penny Auction Solutions filed a SEC Form S-1 in February 2011 outlining its proposed business model. Though it has limited funds at present, it hopes to tap into capital from a group that is prepared to invest in it under certain circumstances.

 COMMON CENTS

Venture Capital
Nothing ventured, nothing gained, right? That's how venture capitalists see it. They don't throw money at just anything. According to the National Venture Capital Association, VCs focus on firms developing significant innovations, such as software, pharmaceuticals, and, yes, new models for consumer sales. Unless a company is poised for significant growth, though, a VC won't invest. Penny auctions attracted big players early – Wellington Partners and August Capital put tens of millions into now-defunct Swoopo. VCs have been less attractive of late.

In its filing, Penny Auction Solutions sees mobile and phone platforms as the key to success. Its own view, shared on a company PowerPoint posted on its website, is that "personal computers are the slot machines of the 21st century" and "we are positioned to capture these users."

And then there's this: "We believe that mobile phone internet usage is the future of the penny auction market. We believe that we are positioned to participate in this potentially addictive mobile shopping entertainment craze."

Whether Penny Auction Solutions has the right understanding and can make a go of it remains to be seen. Its website is under construction, and its SEC filing included an auditor's statement raising substantial doubts about its ability to continue as a "going concern," a major red flag to any would-be investors.

While mobile may be the future at some level, where penny auctions go is perhaps more about placement than platform and marketing than anything else.

Beckham, whose QuiBids is the dominant industry player, believes fun e-commerce rather than mobile devices is the future.

Hetrick agrees.

"I hate to equate it to a gambler's mentality," Hetrick said. "We're looking for risk-takers who are looking for a good value. We don't want people who expect it for a penny. We want people who are looking for the excitement of the game, who want to compete against other shoppers."

In that respect, penny auctions may be more like Black Friday.

The face of the growing landscape goes to the root of the business model. We'll look more deeply inside that next.

3

FOLLOWING THE MONEY

"Those who manage their way into a crisis are not necessarily the right people to manage their way out of a crisis."
—Physicist Albert Einstein

Change, as may well be said, ain't what it used to be.

The penny auction landscape is young, even by today's light-speed standard of measurement. Today, changes see whole sectors – from movie rentals to video games – form and transform in a very short time.

Fax machines seem to have come and gone in the blink of an eye. Pagers were ubiquitous and are now a relic. And the list goes on.

Penny auctions burst onto the commercial scene a little more than a decade after eBay was hatched. It has only been since early 2010 that today's major players emerged, meaning long term predictions about its future come with an extremely tight time frame of reference.

Still, the emerging business model for penny auctions to make money, challenges that make it a struggle for some to stay afloat, and macro technology factors driving e-commerce and entertainment together, are becoming clearer. They help us lay a road map for the future and help us better understand the present.

 COMMON CENTS

E-Commerce
You might not think of penny auctions as e-commerce, but that's exactly what they are. They sell bids online. You buy stuff. Short for electronic commerce, it encompasses everything from online-only retailers, like Amazon.com and StubHub, to Internet sales from traditional stores like Target and Walmart. It may seem like a fringe player, and to some extent it is. The Census Bureau pegs e-commerce sales at just around 5 percent of all purchases. But that sliver amounted to more than $166 billion in 2010. More than a few pennies.

This is important because a deeper grasp gives bidders like you context as you look for places to play and win, and places to avoid as too risky.

We won't spend too much time here – and if you've had too much context already, feel free to skip ahead. Hang with us, though, and you'll know more about what you face and why.

PILING UP PENNIES

Penny auction sites make money when you buy bids. This is their revenue stream.

As you drive up the pennies on a given auction, you are using bids you have either already paid for, received as some sort of voucher for past purchases, or bought at a likely discount through a winning auction of bids themselves.

Revenue is also obtained when losing bidders buy merchandise under buy-it-now-type arrangements. But such sales, while usually more than retail prices, are not the profit centers that bid sales are, as we'll see.

This is fuel for sites' top line – revenue. The $60 you paid for 100 bids, for example, is transferred to them and they keep it. It's cash in their pocket. Whether you bid or stop bidding, win or lose, doesn't matter. Their money was made when you punched the credit card number into your laptop.

You can get the money back under some circumstances when you request a refund. But for the most part, bidders use the bids or they quit playing before the full purchase is consumed. And your bids can be consumed in lightning fashion through automatic bidding and other site features.

Either way, the purchase of bidpacks or packages of bids – however titled – are the mother's milk for everyone from QuiBids on down. And the sales are easier to make today given the familiarity with buying online.

"The comfort level is higher with the expansion of Internet shopping itself," said Jeremy Hetrick of BidPigs. "Ten years ago, people wouldn't put $10 in for a bidpack."

This is where the revenue side is driven and it is one of the reasons marketing is king. Auction A needs to separate itself from Auction B and get you to go there instead of another place.

Auctions drive this revenue side hard and make sales of bids any way they can. Once you have paid-up bids, you're more likely to stay, play, look around, and return.

It is this dependence on bid purchases that both drives the flow of cash and limits the growth of penny auctions. Email campaigns and bonuses are all focused on getting you to buy bids.

Preferably today.

MAKING A BUNDLE

The first time you do the math, it's jaw dropping.

A $15 bid equals 1,500 pennies or, at 60 cents a bid, or a total of $900 gross for the auction site. Let's say all that fun is over an item that sells for $450 at Best Buy.

If you make that a $30 bid, or 3,000 pennies at 60 cents a pop, you've seen $1,800 go under.

You don't need to be a math major, or even smarter than a fifth grader, to figure that is a good deal for somebody.

Are the sites really making that much money? Well, yes and no.

As we said, they made their money, their revenue, on the sale of the bids. So the $900 or $1,800 mentioned above is revenue that's already "made." It just shows up here as the bids are exercised.

The bigger question we're trying to wrap our arms around is whether the auction sites have a 100- or 200-plus percent margin, or mark-up, over the cost of goods sold. That is, are they getting something themselves for $10 and then turning around and selling it via penny auction for far more than that? If so, even accounting for shipping, staffing, electric bills and the like, it really is a license to print money.

 COMMON CENTS

Margin
Penny auction site owners don't disclose their profit margins, but they undoubtedly keep track more closely than any powerbidder follows a coveted iPad. Keeping this positive is the difference between being in business and being out of merchandise. Arrive at the net profit margin by first figuring net income, which involves adding up all revenues and then subtracts all expenses. Then, divide net income by the revenues and multiply by 100. That number, expressed as a percentage, is the net profit margin.

Going inside the business model, the huge markup – while present on some sales at some times – is not the rule. Auctions can take a loss when items go for literally pennies – and they do. And many auctions are pumped up with bids either given away or obtained as a package with merchandise, meaning you can't just multiply 60 cents times each penny to get the value of what's consumed.

Add to that sales and marketing expenses, which increasingly involve costly television and other mass methods, and tech costs for analytics and tracking.

Penny auction websites can also see the expense side hit through the buy-it-now option. These safety nets are created to protect you from seeing your bid investment (which you're already made; remember the credit card number) vaporized as you bid like crazy to land a wristwatch.

To keep you playing in this sandbox, the exchange is the protection of being able to see the value of your bids applied toward the purchase – at retail – of the wristwatch, to use the previous example.

While the "retail price" is more than a careful shopper would pay at the store, it's relatively close, with whatever mark-up the website makes not likely offsetting the value of the bids it applies for the buyer to the item.

 COMMON CENTS

Retail

Do you pay the sticker price for clothes or for a car? Whatever you buy, you likely aim to get a deep discount, with the cut rate well off the price on the tag. The retail price is how much sellers are advised by the manufacturer to charge in stores. It is a benchmark of sorts and one that, depending on the item, may be close to or a good bit away from what you pay. The retail price is listed next to selections on penny auction sites. If you don't win the item by bidding, many sites give you the option to buy what you missed at retail.

Bottom line: Successful sites make money, but not as much as you may think. QuiBids pegs its net profit margin at 5 to 10 percent, which would put it in the realm of insurance brokers, auto parts stores, and hotels, according to Yahoo! Finance.

QuiBids figures can't be independently verified, as they are not a public company and their financials are not made available. Comparisons with principals of other sites and available data suggest the range to a 10 percent-plus margin is likely a reasonable estimate.

WIDENING THE MARGIN

The key to greater profitability for sites – big and small – is to minimize expenses as they maximize revenue, right?

As we saw earlier, revenue comes when sites successfully convince you they offer the best deals and you buy a set of bids from them.

Revenue growth, then, is most dependent on marketing success. This relates to everything from how easy it is to understand and use a website to how well a site owner converts email solicitations and how attractive the range of products is.

That is, revenue depends on stuff that's going to cost sites money.

A key to widening the profit margin, then, is getting merchandise for less, particularly if they have to spend more and more money to get and keep you on their site.

Penny auction sites can get items for less than retail prices, particularly when they deal with higher volumes as larger sites. They are not manufacturers, though, and a $25 Target gift card is still going to cost near the sticker price.

Some, like QuiBids, have multiple relationships with vendors and have many items shipped directly from companies or third-party warehouses. This keeps them from sucking up cash with large amounts of inventory and paying employees to keep them.

The down side is drop-shipping carries a closer-to-retail price for goods, meaning volume of sales are needed to keep the margin high.

That has not been a problem so far for QuiBids, which launched a site for Canadians in August 2011 and Australians in September 2011.

By contrast, SkoreIt! controls most everything it sells. This allows them to get items for better prices even as they handle some inventory costs. The risk they carry is making sure items are ones that sell, and sell in the aggregate for multiples that will cover the costs.

Time will tell which model is the standard and whether either or both are sustainable.

PENNY POINTS

The Road Ahead
The penny auction landscape is changing. Here are some key points to keep in mind:

1. The field is narrowing. Contrary to critical reports and drive-by analysis, penny auctions are not a borderline gambling method giving owners a simple license to print money. If they were, the field would be even more littered with players, with larger ones kicking up more water in the pool. It is not very easy to make it.

2. Start-ups need their own plan. The early attraction of venture capital to some start-ups has waned as the challenges of long-term survival become apparent and early name brands like Swoopo go under. Self-financing to get and stay going may be necessary.

3. Marketing is king. Competition for buyers everywhere – from online to corner retail – is strong. So is the demand for bargains and deals. Penny auctions provide an attractive option for some and can still offer killer buys. But they must be about more than deals to survive, since a cut-rate option is around every corner. The best sites separate themselves through successful marketing to keep bidders coming back.

4. Analytics is king, too. Behind the wall, the best operators place auctions and screen players to churn bids and winners. There is some caution on the player side of that, which we'll discuss later.

FUNDAMENTAL FUN

One more thing before we get more into the nuts and bolts of participating in penny auctions.

Think FarmVille.

As the penny auction landscape flattens out, the sites themselves are looking for new avenues of expansion. This involves raising revenues through the sales of more bids and moving the model itself beyond a reliance on selling bids.

"It's not just about the auctions," said QuiBids' Matt Beckham. "There is some fun now, but the majority of our users are looking for the excitement of the deal. We think there is a lot more to be had."

For inspiration, Beckham and others are looking at people like Mark Pincus, the founder of Zynga and Facebook games like FarmVille.

A profile in the June 2011 edition of *Vanity Fair* magazine examined Pincus and his company, which has been valued at more than $10 billion and boasts 150 million unique monthly users. Its 2010 revenues were nearly $600 million.

Michael Pachter, a video game analyst at Wedbush Securities, said the exploding success of Facebook, the ubiquitous social networking site, owed something to an inventor of online games and fun.

"Is Facebook's success because of Zynga, or is Zynga a success because of Facebook?" Pachter asked. "The answer is both. But the truth is that it's a delicate eco-system."

Among the successful points of FarmVille, analysts said, is they're easy to play, encourage you to play through a sense of ownership, and even penalize you through dead crops and such when you don't come back to play regularly.

In a world of online entertainment, they are a break that people are seemingly hungry for.

Kids, after all, love the plush-toy Webkinz and take-care-of-it websites. They also play games and adopt their own pet monsters on Moshi Monsters.

Knowledgeable people we talked with had a common theme: More fun is to come. In October 2011, for example, QuiBids launched a games feature. It mixes winning bids with treasure hunts, pirates, and the chance to win more bids.

Just what the whole games and auction landscape will look like in six months or 16 months remains to be seen, but changes are no doubt coming.

In the meantime, we're going to look next at the auctions themselves and the best practices you can employ to do well.

That is, after all, a little more fun than the alternative.

PENNY WISE

4

FUNDAMENTALS & FORMATS

"You can't extend, or go beyond any point musically,
without the basic fundamentals."
—Musician Chico Hamilton

The first look around a busy penny auction site is memorable. You might relate it to the iconic picture of a flustered stock trader. Surrounded by more than a dozen computer screens, he seems to be falling short in making sense of an all-too confusing world.

We know what it's like.

The array of timers. The changing penny amounts. The smart looking pictures of tech merchandise and name brands. It's a little like a carnival gone mad.

No doubt the multiple things happening at once are part of the attraction of entertainment shopping. After all, we are an increasingly multi-tasking society. We can walk, chew gum, and do both while we're texting our brother-in-law and ordering a burger at Sonic.

What did you say?

Oh, right. Setting aside the various studies of the brain and how much we can efficiently absorb at one time, the multi-platform screen of most any penny auction site isn't really beyond our grasp. With some quick definitions, we'll try to make a little more sense of it all.

The next several chapters key on the focus of this book: Helping you win penny auctions more often, save more dollars, and avoid common mistakes.

First, we'll focus on the basics, reviewing a bit for the benefit of anxious readers who skipped ahead to here.

The shift from beginner to expert doesn't happen overnight, and you can't successfully focus on strategy until you understand the fundamentals.

PENNY AUCTIONS 101

Every penny auction starts with an opening price of one cent, hence the name penny auction. Every bid adds another penny to the auction price.

Sounds simple, right? It is, except for a small catch.

Unlike traditional auctions, penny auction sites sell you bids before participating. The bids range anywhere from 25 cents to a $1 each and can be non-refundable.

Several bid purchase options at QuiBids.com

You have to pay to play. This makes penny auctions different from traditional auction and online sales websites like eBay.

This distinction has led some to instead call the format a pay-per-bid auction or a bidding fee auction.

Some sites are willing to give you a few free bids just for signing up, but eventually you'll need to purchase a bid package if you want to be competitive. With bids in hand, you're legal and can start bidding. (Though we encourage you to keep reading first. We explain bid packages in Chapter 5 and strategies for bidding in Chapter 6.)

Along with a unique approach to bidding is a different approach to sales: A timer that counts down toward zero but is constantly changing and sometimes goes up.

When the clock is running, the auction is open. When less than a minute remains, most sites add time to the clock (usually 10 to 15 seconds) for each bid placed. This feature is the online equivalent of an auctioneer asking for a higher bid.

The winner is the last person to place a bid before the clock expires. A lucky person could place one bid and win the auction at a price of a penny. It happens. Not very often, though. Nearly every auction ends well above the few cents you may have seen on television commercials.

 COMMON CENTS

Clock

Like a college basketball game, the clock in penny auctions can seem to go on forever. Sometimes called a timer, this is a key device to keep your eye on as you bid. As it gets close to crunch time, the clock runs down to near zero. It is extended every time you or someone else registers a bid, typically from 5 to 20 seconds. All standard penny auctions have a clock. Each auction in this context runs like a conventional auction in that it keeps going as long as people are wanting to buy. In this respect, penny auctions differ from eBay-type buying and selling.

If you were to track penny auctions for $25 gift cards (and if you are interested in these, you should be tracking them), you may notice these auctions often end in the range of 20 to 100 pennies, or 20 cents to $1. And up.

If you are a winning bidder of the gift card for, say, 75 cents, your actual cost is the winning bid plus shipping. That may be $2 or more.

Remember to factor in the cost of any bids you paid for, too. Your penny bids were not free unless they were all given to you at sign-up or through another bonus or as part of winning another item.

BUY-IT-NOW

How bad a deal it is when you lose depends on the auction and your needs.

Losers can and often do walk away empty-handed. Since each bidder uses paid (often non-refundable) bids to participate, losing can be quite costly.

Because the penny auction model allows for only one winner, websites have to find creative ways to get and retain new bidders. There are more than a fair share of losers for every winner.

Part of this involves creating a floor to keep losers from losing everything: An option to buy the items at retail and even credit the cost of your paid-for bids toward the purchase price.

Back to the $25 gift card. If in this instance the bidder placed 15 bids costing 75 cents each, they would have already invested the equivalent of $11.25 in the auction. With a bid-to-buy or buy-it-now option, the site will sell the card to the loser at face value – or another $13.75 – plus shipping.

As we said earlier, this is a drain on penny auctions' profitability. But it also can keep bidders around and buying bid packages, the real cash cow, and reduces this risk often associated with penny auctions. The worst-case scenario is paying the retail price, plus shipping, for an item you can use, give away, or sell.

One more thing: The buy-in-now option can make auctions tougher to win. If other auction participants want the same gift card as you, they may be more willing to bid since they have the safety net option.

No good deed goes unpunished.

 COMMON CENTS

Buy-It-Now
There's one winner in the traditional penny auction model. This is good for the person landing the MacBook Pro for a fraction of its cost, but everybody else is shut out. That's too much risk for many bidders. A buy-it-now feature typically gives losing bidders a set amount of time to purchase the item they lost anyway at the retail price, with the cost reduced by the value of purchased bids. Notice we didn't say all bids. Bids you get as credits, incentives, as part of other auctions, etc., don't carry an out-of-pocket value and don't factor into discounts off the price.

BIDS AND VOUCHERS

While bids are typically purchased in packages, some are gained as bonuses for bidding milestones you pass, your referrals of new bidders, and your own signing up.

These no-direct-cost bids, commonly referred to as vouchers, can also be gained through winning something like a gift card (e.g. - $15 Target card plus 10 voucher bids) or a bid package that is sold at auction rather than purchased directly by you from the site.

We covered some of this ground earlier: Sites make their money when you buy bid packages. The vouchers, then, are a cost of doing business akin to a retailer giving you bonus bucks to spend on a new dress or suit.

Accordingly, the same benefits don't always accrue.

For example, the buy-it-now feature we just covered doesn't typically extend the same dollar-for-dollar credit for voucher bids as ones you bought directly. When you lose out on that $25 gift card using all voucher bids, the site will credit you $0 toward the card.

The benefit of voucher bids is you can move auctions up a penny just as you can with other bids without cost. The downside is you get no credit later should you lose and want to get credit for what you consumed in losing bids.

The way the sites look at it, you're not out of pocket so they won't be either.

Keep that in mind.

 COMMON CENTS

Free Bids
There are lots of ways to get bids without forking over a credit card number. Some come as a bonus for your registration info, others come from referring a friend or after hitting a threshold for the number of bids used. You can also get bids through an auction, sometimes called voucher bids, such as a gift card that includes 10 bids for the winner, or in an outright auction of bids. These are very important to accumulate as they let you be a player with far less money out of pocket. The terms free bids and vouchers are sometimes used interchangeably.

RULES, MERCHANDISE, AND PLAYING IT SAFE

Along with things like timers and rising penny auctions, sites have a couple other key elements you need to examine.

First, check out what is for sale. Some sites specialize in gift cards and smaller items. Others add higher value items to the mix, including the newest tech gadgets, designer accessories, and more.

Ask yourself what you're looking for most. Examine the site to see what it sells more of and what it doesn't have at all. Look around and see what fits you.

Second, scout the site for contact information and other details. Make sure this information is easily accessible and check it out. Some sites have helpful Frequently Asked Question areas and places for user comments. Read the questions and answers. Do they pass your own smell test?

As with anything else, you need to keep your critical thinking hat on. Not all comments can be assumed to be from real buyers, depending on the site.

Look at the larger picture. If a site seems to lack contacts, displays odd clock movements, or otherwise seems uncomfortable, then find another site. There are lots of options.

This leads again into the Big Question: Am I on a legitimate site?

Chapter 7 will help you learn how to spot red flags. You need to keep your eyes open for shill bidding or sites that fail to deliver.

Shill bidding can take a variety of forms, but it simply means an individual – in this case, a site owner – is fraudulently raising the price of the items up for auction. It happens in traditional auctions, eBay, and penny auctions alike.

A few sites have been caught using fake computer bidders (often called "bots") to make auctions appear more competitive than they really are and to ensure they don't take a loss. This is against the law.

OTHER FORMATS

In the eyes of some entrepreneurs, the traditional penny auction serves as a launching pad for additional auction formats and new entertainment shopping platforms.

Using the traditional penny auction as a backdrop, developers continue to push the limits and introduce new auction variations.

As you begin to navigate the landscape on your own, you will undoubtedly encounter some of these new auctions types. It's worth taking a look before we move on.

>> Blind Auctions >>
Blind auctions were designed to make auctions unpredictable.

They work the same way as a traditional penny auction, but all user names are hidden. Each bidder is assigned a random ID (usually a sequence of numbers) and the user names are not revealed until the auction is over.

Pros: Users can't use the reputation of their bidding name to intimidate other bidders. Blind auctions level the playing field.

Cons: Users have a difficult time strategizing since they don't know what types of bidders they are competing against.

>> Lowest Unique Bid Auctions >>

Similar to the penny auction, lowest unique bid auctions require users to pay-per-bid. However, several features set these auctions apart. First, lowest unique bid sites remove the timer from the equation. Instead of actively competing against other users and the clock, bidders strategize by guessing a price within a preset range.

For example, an auction for a $50 gift card may have a pre-defined price range of 1 cent to 75 cents. Users are competing against each other to guess the lowest price that nobody else guesses. Each guess costs one bid. If users multiple users guessed 1, 2, and 4 cents, but only one user guessed 3 cents, the 3 cent guess is the lowest unique bid and that individual is the winner.

Pros: Ending prices for lowest unique bid auctions are always low. Bidders don't have to worry about timers or fierce, instantaneous competition.

Cons: Lowest unique bid auctions require a great deal of strategy. Users can burn through their bids quickly learning how to play.

🏆 PENNY POINTS

What Does it Cost?

Yes, you can get items for a penny. Well, almost a penny. You need to take several costs into account when doing your own math."

1. Bids. How much you paid for your bids is a key factor. If you paid 60 cents each and bid 20 times to fetch the gift card, you used up $12.

2. Price. You will pay the winning bid price, whether that's 1 cent or $10.

3. Shipping & Handling. The gift card won't arrive in the mail for free. The site will charge you something to mail it. Include that in figuring what your item cost.

4. Loss. If you use up 20 bids and lose, that does not come without a price. Keep track of what you spend and use.

5. Buy-It-Now. If you exercise a buy-it-now option, paid-for bids will be credited to your purchase. Free or voucher bids will not. Take all this into account when figuring your ups and downs.

>> Reverse Auctions >>

Reverse auctions work the same way as a traditional penny auction, but the price for each item goes down with every bid placed. It's a penny auction in reverse.

Pros: Every bid placed actually lowers the price of the item up for auction. If the auction price goes into a negative price range, some reverse auction sites actually pay the winning bidder the difference.

Cons: Most penny auctions begin with a starting price of 1 cent. Reverse auctions have a higher starting price.

>> Reserve Auctions >>

Reserve auctions allow the site owner to set a "reserve price," or the minimum acceptable price for the item. If the reserve is not met, the auction is over and the cost of bids are refunded. If the item is sold, though, the bids are lost. Some reserve auctions limit the use of the timer, only starting it after the reserve is hit. The reserve price is not known ahead of time to bidders.

Pros: Reserve auctions require less commitment from bidders, since auctions that don't hit the reserve result in refunded bids. Bidders can let others invest their resources before committing to the battle, which can be more cost-effective.

Cons: The reserve auction model tends to favor auction owners more than bidders. The owner can ensure the site doesn't take a loss, but bidders hoping to clear the reserve price can't guarantee the same.

>> Seat Auctions >>

Seat auctions require bidders to buy "seats" in order to compete. A limited number of seats are available. Those buying seats bid against each other at the set date and time for the auction. Bidders typically get an unlimited number of bids to use.

Pros: In a seat auction, bidders know the exact number of opponents they are up against. Limited competition means a higher probability of winning.

Cons: Seat auctions are often expensive to participate in. Most sites charge a cash entry fee or require a large chunk of bids in order for bidders to reserve their spot.

5

BUYING & STUDYING

"When I was younger, studying classical music, I really had to put in the time. Three hours a day is not even nice – you have to put in six."
—Actress / Musician Alicia Keys

Penny auctions are entertainment with consequences. Participating with no strategy and collecting more than a few failed auction attempts will probably leave you doubting the entertainment element as you contemplate the consequences.

Experienced bidders say the thrill of scoring an unbelievable deal is worth the effort that goes into it. But they've had to learn a few tough lessons along the way.

As with most learning, success requires an up-front investment. The good news is you've already invested some by reading chapters 1-4.

With fundamentals and auction formats in the back of your mind, shift your focus to the three elements you need to win penny auctions – time, strategy, and a bit of luck.

As you do, center on how you can use your time and apply what you read to developing an intentional strategy for competing in online penny auctions. This will help you to lessen the impact of the bidding elements you cannot control.

We talked with experienced bidders willing to lay their cards on the table as a way of welcoming you into the world of entertainment shopping. Their tips are folded into the next few chapters. Take the advice as a buffet of sorts. Fill your strategy plate with the ideas you like and leave the other tips for the next guy.

In doing so, determine what type of bidder you want to become before ever placing a bid. By developing an intentional strategy up front, you'll be more likely to avoid silly beginner mistakes, such as jumping from auction to auction with no real target, using an auto-bid feature carelessly, or burning up your first bids competing against a bidding shark.

Now that you've put the training wheels on the bike, it's time to start peddling.

CHOOSE THE RIGHT USER NAME

Your user name becomes the identity you're associated with throughout the penny auction community. As you win and participate, you will become noticed, particularly on smaller sites with less frequent auctions.

If you don't understand why this is a big deal, think about the town you live in. Is it fair to say certain names dredge up negative or positive associations? Depending on what side of the sports or political fence you're on, names like Alex Rodriguez and Bill Clinton probably evoke strong emotions, or at least an association with something.

Penny auctions are like your town. As you bid, users will begin to associate your name with your actions. Opposing bidders will know how seriously they should take you based on the reputation you've developed in previous auctions. The smaller the town/penny auction, the more you're noticed.

In the penny auction community, your name is everything. You want others to believe you have a consistent strategy and you're serious about winning. Over time, you'll need to develop a track record that backs up those assumptions.

While not as critical on larger penny auction sites that see hundreds of auctions a day, some bidders will begin tracking your bidding habits and use those habits against you. We'll explain how to track other bidders in Chapter 7.

Choosing the right name is important because your name is the only real impression you can make on your competitors. As you bid and win, you want to leave losing bidders with a name they will remember and avoid.

Your long-term goal is to build a solid bidding reputation that accompanies your name. Choose wisely.

 **PENNY POINTS**

Forge an Identity
Pick a user name that reflects your personality, interests, or the bidding strategy you plan to employ. The name itself isn't nearly as important as the reputation you build along with it.

1. Make it memorable. These are all real bidders you may encounter along the way. Each has a bidding reputation associated with their name.

- Intimidating names - Bid2Dead, NOTGONNASTOP, itsMINEnow
- Humorous names - SaveDemBids, cwazyrabbit, angryracoon
- Unique names - amcoffee, hifiken, 65chevy, dzignr_tastz

2. Avoid personally-identifying information. Your user name should not be your email address, full name, phone number or anything else that would allow users to contact you directly.

3. Be original. Sometimes users try to steal the name and reputation of stronger bidders. Stealing usernames doesn't go over well in the penny auction community.

SHOP FOR YOUR FIRST BID PACKAGE

Penny auction websites crave new bidders.

As we discussed, the penny auction business model relies on you buying bids and using them against other bidders on a regular basis. The more aggressive the competition, the better the bottom line.

For owners, that is.

But owners also face the challenge of regularly attracting new bidders. Consequently, many sites offer special discounts for users buying their first package of bids, often called bidpacks. Since you can usually only be a new bidder once, cash in on these promotions.

Perks can range from a doubling of your first bid package purchase to bidpacks discounted by 10 to 20 percent. Some even throw in a few free bids for good measure.

 **PENNY POINTS**

Package Your Bidpack Purchase
Sites periodically offer package discounts. Be ready for these opportunities and cash in while you can. Here are some other tips:

1. Stay connected with discount sites. Some websites act as clearinghouses for bid package discounts and deals. Check out the Piggybank section at the end of the book for a rundown of options.

2. Buy in bulk. Just like huge retailers, you can save when you buy a lot at one time. Most sites lower the cost-per-bid when you purchase a larger packages.

3. Follow sites on Twitter and Facebook. Sites sometimes use social networks to announce giveaways, contests, and other promotions.

Most bids have an expiration date of six months to a year, so be sure to check the Terms & Conditions or Help section of a website to familiarize yourself with their bid policies.

You'll soon be going up against experienced bidders who already know their way around. Maximizing the number of bids in your initial purchase means more competitive power for you and, hopefully, more return on your initial investment.

If a site isn't offering any new user discounts and you otherwise like the auction set-up and options, send an email and ask for an incentive for registering.

Penny auctions are always looking to expand their user base, so the power is temporarily in your hands.

When you register on a new site, view your first bid package as a crucial investment. Never miss out on a worthwhile promotional opportunity. If bids cost 75 cents each on a given site and you can get them for 45 cents, you gain a cost-effective advantage that your opponents may not have.

Before you purchase your first bidpack at a bargain price, though, spend a little time to develop a solid game plan for using those bids.

RESEARCH BEFORE YOU BID

If you dreaded homework in high school, we have some bad news: There are two additional assignments you should complete before bidding on any penny auction website.

You can take off your training wheels and skip the assignments if you choose, but know your choices may affect your performance. Success requires an investment of time along with some dollars.

If you're reading this book and you've participated in fantasy football, for example, you know a little bit of research goes a long way. The best fantasy team "owners" obsess over details and enact a solid game plan for team success. The game plan may need to be altered when the star running back tears his hamstring, but it's easier to modify on the fly than it is to create a plan out of thin air – especially when a clock is ticking.

Penny auctions are a game. The most successful competitors familiarize themselves with the playing field and their opponents before they ever step into the arena.

In our conversations with bidders, we took note of a recurring theme: Preparation is key.

Anthony Rosner, a cautious but successful bidder from Indiana, emphasized the importance of research.

Bidders – especially beginners – should "check ended auctions and identify patterns," he said. This includes the winners, winning bid prices, and user names.

Raul Ochoa, a semi-aggressive bidder from Texas, emphasized preparation as well. When he started bidding, he went head to head with some of the toughest bidders in the game. Needless to say, he learned who he shouldn't go against after the fact.

"Always do your research," he said. "The best way to win is do your research and build your strategy from there."

How do you do research? Read on.

ASSIGNMENT #1: REVIEW PAST AUCTION DATA

Most penny auction websites have an "Ended Auctions" section. Start there.

For this assignment, sift through a week's worth of ended auctions. This process will give you a rough idea of what items sell for on that respective site.

 COMMON CENTS

Historical Prices
In determining when to participate in an auction, it's important to know what like items have sold for in the past. This gives you a good barometer for what an item may sell for the next time around. These are available from several online sources, each claiming to track sales at a range of sites. It's worth taking a look at those. But they are not comprehensive. The best way to track is doing the hard work yourself of watching how sales track on a particular site. Keep a spreadsheet and watch the flow of the auction for yourself on items you want to land.

Note to overachievers and data-lovers: Feel free to look through a month's worth of auctions for a broader sampling or head over to a site like AllPennyAuctions.com to get detailed site and auction information. More on that in Chapter 7.

As you review ended auctions, pay close attention to what time each auction ended and the final price for each item.

If you notice $25 gift cards typically end in the 40-cent range between 1 and 5 p.m., and the 60 cent range between 5 and 11 p.m., make a note that afternoon auctions on that website generally go cheaper and you should expect the final price to be somewhere around 40 to 60 cents.

Anticipate anomalies along the way – gift cards that end for 3 cents or 90 cents, for example. But as a general rule, put some confidence in the pattern of selling prices on the site you're studying. This information will help you set reasonable expectations and use your paid bids intelligently.

Also take note of bidders who seem to win regularly. If certain names keep appearing as auction winners, this may be an indication you don't want to bid against them right away. It may also be an indication their strategy works well on that particular site.

Figure out what those bidders are doing to win and you'll be one step closer to swimming with the sharks.

ASSIGNMENT #2: WATCH AUCTIONS

As the penny auction timer beckons you to bid, ignore the bright lights and patiently observe what's happening.

Figure out what items you want to target as a new bidder and start to monitor bidder behavior on those auctions. Take note of strategies that seem to work and learn from the mistakes of others.

This is a crucial step for success. Ignore it at your own risk.

Mike Dionne, an aggressive bidder with TV and computer wins under his belt, can testify to the importance of this assignment.

Dionne was first introduced to penny auctions by a friend who was kind enough to teach him the ropes. Still, he took some precautions before jumping in, developing his own strategy over many weeks of watching auctions and not bidding.

Once confident, Dionne started to participate in auctions for the first time and has had a successful run. Starting out on Beezid.com, he eventually branched out to smaller sites where he continues to do well. He reports taking home about three times as much in merchandise as he spends.

Part of his success is no doubt a direct result of preliminary research and continued patience.

ADOPT A BIDDING STRATEGY

If you take the time to complete the two assignments, you can use your observations to decide on a bidding strategy.

Your strategy is the consistent approach your employ to win on sites. Some strategies work great on large sites but fail miserably on smaller ones. Others may simply not fit your personality.

If you crave action and simply can't be patient, you'll probably struggle with penny auctions overall. Some strategies, though, can serve to mitigate this trait while others will serve to give you an incredibly short bidding career.

If you learn to apply the right strategy, on the right website, and at the right time, you will position yourself to win more often, save more dollars, and avoid common mistakes.

In Chapter 6, we further develop some strategies and tips.

6
STRATEGIES & TIPS

"If you're not making mistakes, you're not taking risks, and that means you're not going anywhere. The key is to make errors faster than the competition, so you have more chances to learn and win."
—Best-selling author John W. Holt Jr.

You will lose some auctions. There is no fail-safe way to always win.

This doesn't eliminate opportunities for success. For inspiration, look at the all-star third baseman who fails at hitting the ball seven out of every 10 times and is a superstar.

The homework assignments from the previous chapter will help you reduce the risk of failure, not eliminate it.

The choice of a bidding strategy is also a crucial step on your road to winning more often, saving more dollars, and avoiding common mistakes. You need to adopt one that is successful for the site you are frequenting and a match for your personality and approach.

The selection is important because it will give you focus and consistency, two elements successful penny auction bidders use to their advantage.

In assessing the overall success rates of various strategies, we've created a Pretty Penny Success Meter. The scale goes from 1 (likely failure) to 5 (likely success). We've laid out two scores. For smaller sites, think a few auctions a day; for larger ones, think lots of things happening at once.

EARLY BIRD

Most penny auction websites post upcoming auctions a few days in advance. Some bidders like to research which items go for less and place bids early in the game in the hope of avoiding tougher competition.

Typically, bidders using this strategy are looking for an easy deal, not a bidding battle. They are willing to yield a few bids but often fold when real competition arrives.

This type of approach aims to land the big deal. The gift cards that sell for a nickel – and there are those that do – are won by this method. It is also the one that relies most heavily on plain luck.

Players who want deals and no risk gravitate to this strategy. Perhaps wins every once in a while can keep them going.

Where to Use
The early bird strategy is most effective with low value items or auctions that take place during non-peak hours on smaller websites. On larger websites, the early bid strategy yields occasional success on low demand items.

While bidders are fighting over high-ticket electronics or popular gift cards, early bidders can scoop up some of the more random product offerings, like an OXO plastic bag holder.

Strengths
Bidding early won't cost you big bucks, so in that respect it is low-risk. An auction win resulting from a few early bids can be a great deal.

Weaknesses

This strategy rarely works. Bidders have to hope site traffic and attention are low at the time of the auction. Bidders who rely on this strategy also weaken the bargaining power of their user name. If other bidders learn they are only willing to place 3 or 4 bids in pursuit of an item, they are more likely to challenge the early bid.

PRETTY PENNY SUCCESS METER

TAG AND DEFEND

This strategy is a more successful hybrid of the Early Bird approach. It is also the most prominent approach in play today.

As soon as a new auction goes live, some bidders like to show an early interest by "tagging" the auction with a first bid. By tagging, we mean placing the first bid on an auction with the mindset you are claiming that auction. It's almost like putting your flag on the moon.

This move tells other users the tagger wants the item and is willing to invest bids early as a way of proving it. As other bidders arrive and place a later bid, the first bidder returns and cancels it out with another bid as a way of defending what they've tagged.

This differs from the Early Bird approach in that the bidder who tags doesn't just hope to go unnoticed. They plan to fight the battle and come out on top. As they build a strong tag and defend reputation, their tag becomes a cost-effective way to discourage competition.

Where to Use
The tag and defend strategy seems to work best on smaller websites where everybody knows your name (that's for you, *Cheers* fans). It also seems to be most effective with smaller ticket items, such as low-value gift cards and electronics with a retail value of less than $50. If that's your market, this may be for you.

Strengths
When a user places their first bid and establishes a track record of defending their tagged auctions, most average bidders avoid the conflict and look to another place they can win more easily.

Also, some bidders wait for an auction to reach a certain threshold before they start bidding. Early aggression may allow a user to "get the worm" while the other birds are still sleeping.

Weaknesses
A first-bid reputation tends to carry less weight on a larger site. It's easy to tag and defend an auction with three potential participants. It's much harder to defend an auction with 30 active participants. Proponents of this strategy often have to take a different approach on larger penny auction websites.

LARGER SITES   SMALLER SITES

3

1   5

FAIL   WIN

PRETTY PENNY SUCCESS METER

POWERBIDDING

Powerbidding is the most aggressive bidding strategy. Think of the childhood game "King of the Hill" and you get the idea.

Powerbidders look to strike fear in the hearts of their opponents. Anytime a user cancels out their initial bid, the powerbidder immediately places another bid to retain their status as the de facto leader. This action is sometimes referred to as throttling.

Many sites maintain limits on the number of auctions a single registered bidder can win over the course of a month or so. This can limit the ability of powerbidders to take over a site. It can also make periodic "limit-buster" auctions – which are thrown open to any and all participants – particularly competitive.

Where to Use

Most penny auction websites have powerbidders, but this strategy seems to be most effective on the small to mid-sized websites. A powerbidding reputation is especially useful for larger ticket items, such as televisions, computers, and digital cameras, on sites where it's easy to keep track of user names.

Strengths

Powerbidding demoralizes bidding opponents and forces them to consider how much they are willing to fight for the item at stake. The short-term goal of powerbidding is to convince other bidders they should quit while they are ahead.

The long term strength of powerbidding is how other bidders take note of dominant user names. Once powerbidders establish a reputation that they will go the distance, they often score big ticket items with less resistance.

Also worth noting: Powerbidders rarely bid against each other. When they do, it's a sight to be seen.

COMMON CENTS

Powerbidders

Track penny auctions for any length of time and you'll find them. Powerbidders are willing to spend whatever it takes to win. They do that to prove a point to anyone who is watching: PowerBidder765 will not lose. They do this as part of a long-term strategy. The idea is a few losses to scare off the others will score cheaper items down the road. It's the big dog telling the little dogs to stay out of his way. Unless you aim to be a big dog, too, you cannot beat them easily. You can learn to identify them and work within the markers they lay down.

Weaknesses

This strategy requires deep pockets – easily many thousands of dollars up front – or talented bluffing. Effective powerbidders can't back down, which means hundreds of bids can disappear in a matter of minutes as part of the quest to establish or maintain a reputation. Powerbidders sometimes pay significantly more than the retail price of items to maintain their street credibility.

Powerbidders also have to deal with identity theft, in a non-traditional sense. As new sites open, some bidders try to gain an edge by signing up with the user name of various powerbidders and stealing their bidding reputation. That forces powerbidders to ignore their impersonators on other sites or make them pay. It is also hard to maintain a reputation as a powerbidder, particularly as sites add users.

PRETTY PENNY SUCCESS METER

WAR OF ATTRITION

In a war of attrition, the goal is to gradually weaken an opponent until they eventually give up. Bidders using the war of attrition strategy are looking to outlast, rather than dominate, their opponents.

If the powerbidder looks to intimidate, this type of bidder looks to frustrate. If patience is your key virtue, this may be your strategy.

Bidders using this approach often wait until the clock nears zero and then place a single bid that extends the auction. A war of attrition bidder may occasionally use this strategy in a different way. Instead of bidding at the last second, a war of attrition bidder might wait until all last-second bids come in and then cancel out everyone else's bid a few seconds after the clock resets.

This is different than the powerbidding strategy, which seeks to immediately cancel out any high bidders and uses bids more haphazardly.

This type of bidder isn't looking for a lucky, under-the-radar win. Instead, they patiently manage their bids until everyone else decides to rest their bidding finger.

Where to Use
This strategy can be used on virtually any site, in any auction. The goal is always the same: Slowly wear opponents down and survive the flurry of contenders to win.

Strengths
In competitive auctions, it's easy to get caught up in the excitement and bid with emotion rather than intellect. The war of attrition approach is driven by tactical speed rather than emotion. This selective form of bidding allows bidders to conserve their resources while other bidders consume theirs.

Weaknesses

This is a time-intensive strategy. Bidders who employ it need to have an open schedule and plenty of patience. It can extend an auction an hour or much more. A war of attrition is particularly painful to the losers. Practitioners need to prepare for the backlash, especially from angry powerbidders. Since this is an easy strategy for others to replicate, attrition bidders shouldn't be surprised if this same technique is used against them in retaliation.

PRETTY PENNY SUCCESS METER

AUTO-BIDDING

This strategy is based on calculated, impersonal bidding. Some sites allow for this through an auto-bid feature. Users decide how many bids they want to spend, giving the automated feature constraints to follow.

Bidders using the auto-bidding strategy to the fullest extent never place a manual bid. They allow the site to bid on their behalf for the duration of the auction, removing brains from the bidding equation and replacing personal judgment with artificial intelligence.

For some bidders, this may be a good thing.

Most sites have a column indicating what type of bids each participant is using (manual or automated), so this strategy is easy for others to identify.

We use the term strategy loosely. If played this way for an extended period, the description fits. If it is set up for, say, five bids, it's less a strategy than a coffee break.

 COMMON CENTS

Automatic Bidding

If you're an eBay veteran, you know about the thrill of victory – getting that classic baseball card with a last-second bid – and the agony of defeat – losing that other card when a player you never saw swoops in at the end. With penny auctions, take that thrill and agony and multiply it many times. Because the clock is extended with each bid, there are all kinds of swoops both ways. Automatic bidding, called a BidAgent, Bid-O-Matic, or a variation, does the swooping for you. Be careful, though, it'll swallow up your bids faster than Pac-Man.

Where to Use

The effectiveness of auto-bidding varies. Some experienced bidders swear by it, others avoid it altogether. Some sites have the feature built into their script, choosing to disable it on select auctions. This action by certain site owners indicates the deal-scoring effectiveness of a well-placed autobidder.

Research the strategic value of this feature on a site-by-site basis to decide whether or not auto-bidding would be an intelligent strategy move on that particular site.

Strengths

Using an autobidder can discourage other bidders from committing to an auction. Since opponents can't determine how long the autobidder is set to run, some bidders feel it isn't worth the effort to fight an impersonal force.

Weaknesses

The autobid feature can burn through paid bids rather quickly, making it less cost effective than bidding manually. Some sites also limit the number of bids that can be placed this way, so know the ground rules first.

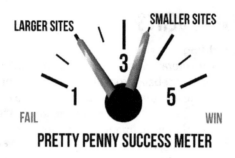

PRETTY PENNY SUCCESS METER

JUMPING

Jumpers wait until most of the auction participants drop out before engaging, or "jumping" into, the competition with both feet.

For example: Bidder A knows the item up for auction typically sells for more than $1, so he lets all the bidders invest significant resources into the battle and waits for the aggressive bidding to slow down.

Once the auction cracks the $1 mark and the competition is down to two or three bidders, he jumps onto the scene with fresh, unused resources and starts bidding aggressively. This leaves the remaining participants with a new opponent to fend off after their initial efforts.

Where to Use

This strategy can be used on any site, but it is best reserved for big sites that can receive a large influx of bidders at any given time or sites with a buy-it-now option.

Those looking to employ the jumping strategy should make sure the auction is in a price range where it may be nearing completion. Bidders who jump too early will probably be jumped later on.

Strengths

From a strategic standpoint, jumping makes a lot of sense. Sites with a forced buy-it-now option won't let bidders compete beyond the retail value of an item, preventing them from spending bids that add up to more than the item itself costs. A jumper can enter the auction when they know many of the early participants are being filtered out via buy-it-now.

Jumping also factors in the limited resources of most auction participants and uses that reality as a strategic advantage.

Weaknesses

Jumping is considered to be a penny auction faux pas within the bidding community, especially on smaller to mid-sized websites. In fact, we can already hear the outrage of some experienced bidders in the distance.

Their logic goes something like this: If Bidder C invests a few hundred dollars and a significant chunk of time into an auction, it's unethical for Bidder A to jump in and "steal" that auction. Bidders often cite a certain respect other bidders should have for their commitment to the battle.

We get it, but a frowned-upon strategy is a strategy nonetheless.

The strategy does have a fatal flaw: Jumpers make enemies left and right, so the long term sustainability of this strategy is an open question. The tag and defend bidder will keep score; the powerbidder will go after you.

PRETTY PENNY SUCCESS METER

TIPS FOR THE ROAD

Before we turn to some more advanced tactics, we'd like to pause and offer some tips as you begin to solidify your approach to penny auctions.

First, be encouraged. You already know more than most first-time bidders.

Second, as you read through the tips, make notes on where you need to focus and what areas of the book you may need to review. Don't head to the advanced approaches until you have a solid grasp on Chapters 4-6 – from the fundamentals to the strategies.

>> Start Small >>

You can have the best game plan in the world, but experience and time should not be undervalued.

Start on websites offering beginner auctions and other safety nets like a buy-it-now option. Avoid big ticket items like televisions and computers until you have a few smaller wins under your belt.

For example, penny auction veteran Raul Ochoa has an iPad, a MacBook Pro, an iPod Touch and other Apple products he can brag about. But his bidding conquests didn't start there.

"After learning who I should and shouldn't go against, I started going for the smaller items," he said. "As I started winning, I began to build myself up to the bigger items. As my name got out there and other bidders knew me, it got easier to win."

Ochoa, who does not describe himself as a powerbidder, emphasizes that "once you get (bidding) experience, people start to respect you."

PENNY POINTS

Track Your Wins
It's easy to get lost in the action. Don't. Keeping an accurate record of your wins will allow you to monitor your own progress and make better strategic decisions later on.

1. Start with a simple spreadsheet. Fire up an Excel document and plug in details with simple formulas.

2. Remember to account for all your costs. As we said in the last chapter, the cost of your bids and packages, the cost of items you win plus shipping, and even things like the cost of this book and other resources should be included.

3. Use the right price. When calculating the other side of the ledger, use the actual price you would have paid for an item rather than the manufacturer's suggested retail price you'll see on the sites. This will paint a more realistic picture.

4. Tap other resources. You'll find resources and examples on ways to track your wins and losses at pennywisethebook.com.

>> Set a Budget, Control Your Emotions >>

These are both important, so consider it one super tip.

If you lay out a budget and plan ahead of time, and if you make a pledge to not let losses and odd bidders get the best of you, the road ahead will be much easier.

Mike Dionne, the bidder we introduced earlier, cautions new bidders to "be patient."

"Emotional bidding leads to major losses," he said, adding his own wallet has suffered as a result of bidding recklessly.

Make sure you hold yourself to a reasonable bidding budget until you have the wins to justify your spending.

>> Read Penny Auction Reviews >>

As disappointing as it may be, there are bad apples in the penny auction industry.

In the last two years, several sites have been caught using shill bidding practices (fake bidders or paid bidders) to drive up auction prices. Other sites have failed to ship wins to their customers and closed unexpectedly.

These sites have proven to be the exception. Still, you should do all you can to avoid a negative experience, such as examining penny auction reviews.

 COMMON CENTS

Bot Bids

The well-dressed guy in the corner wants to buy Aunt Mary's farm, right? Or is he on the payroll of XYZ Auctions to drive up the price? Hiring a plant to place illegitimate bids and provoke others to bid more is an old trick. And it's against the law. In the online world of penny auctions, such a plant comes in the form of robotic bot bids, or shill bidding. This concern undermines the legitimacy of unregulated penny auctions, where it's buyer beware. You may never know if Bear55 is a real person or not, but you can take steps to limit your exposure to bot bids.

Bidder Raul Ochoa advises to "always read reviews of a site, just like you would read reviews for an item you were buying from an online store."

Chapter 10 provides resources to consult before deciding whether to share credit card information.

>> Enjoy the Journey >>

Many penny auction websites brand themselves as entertainment shopping venues. And when you win, the thrill of a great deal is quite entertaining.

Enjoy that experience while it lasts. But balance positives with negatives. Remind yourself even the most powerful bidders fail to win auctions on occasion.

If you're not having fun, take a break from bidding or look for a site that provides you with a better bidding experience.

Now, the training wheels are off and its time for you to ride. If you fall off the bike, come back to this chapter for help.

More advanced tips and advice are up next.

7

STAY AHEAD OF THE GAME

"It has been my observation that most people get ahead during the time that others waste."
—American innovator Henry Ford

Once you win a few auctions, you will discover some of the advantages you had as a newbie start to disappear. Continued success with penny auction depends on your ability to adapt to the ever-changing mix of bidders and website offerings.

Some sites offer a discounted price for bids when you first register. After you capitalize on those opportunities, most introductory bid package deals disappear.

Once you have a few wins under your belt, beginner auctions will also disappear. You'll be forced to compete in intermediate or expert auctions with other experienced bidders.

As a beginner, enjoy the perks up front and then prepare yourself to swim with the sharks.

Chapters 4, 5 and 6 are equipping chapters. They help you find initial success in the competitive shopping arena.

We'll now offer some suggestions to keep you from being eaten alive and on the road to winning more often, saving more dollars, and avoiding common mistakes.

MATCH SITES TO YOUR FOCUS

The sites you choose to play make or break you in the long run. As a general rule, frequent sites that give you the greatest opportunity to win and the sites meeting the bidding goals you set for yourself.

For example, if your goal is to win lower value gift cards for restaurants, gas, or other retail establishments, smaller penny auction sites can be a better focus. These primarily offer auctions that meet your objective.

It can be easier to win the gift cards you want on a smaller site. There is usually less bidding competition and more opportunities for you to capitalize on the reputation of your bidding name – assuming you have a solid track record to back up that name.

But you can get even more intentional.

In Chapter 5, we told you to register a user name, maximize your first bid package purchase, and research the auctions before jumping in.

Remember, too: The most successful bidders choose where they are going to play, not just how they are going to play.

Review the data for ended gift card auctions on Sites A, B, and C. Average the auction results to figure out which site is selling those gift cards for the lowest price and start bidding there first. Why bid on Site C when Site A clearly has the better deals?

Another way to stay ahead of the game is to pay close attention to bid prices.

In the long run, how much you pay per bid is important. If Site A has lower average ending prices but their bids cost $1 each, the numbers may be a bit misleading – especially if Sites B and C are both selling bids for 60 cents each.

On the other side, if your goal is to reel in big ticket items, the larger penny auction sites will probably serve you best. Small sites often lack the capital necessary to auction TVs, computers, and iPads on a regular basis, so you shouldn't waste your time there.

Large sites are typically more difficult to win on, as you are forced to fight off a constant influx of bidders who are all aiming for the same big ticket item. But success on big sites usually has a higher payout. One good computer win has a net profit of many gift cards combined.

Since large sites often run auctions 24 hours a day, you'll want to figure out the ideal times to bid and avoid the temptation to bid when traffic is at its height. Bidding at the right time also sets experts apart from beginners. The right time varies by site, so research should guide your decisions.

Common sense is another factor in determining the right time to bid. If you look during your lunch break, remind yourself you're not the only one who gets a lunch break. On the other hand, if you work on the east coast and the site you're playing at primarily markets to the west coast three hours behind, your lunch break may be a great time to bid.

Some bidders set their alarm for 3 a.m. because the large sites they frequent seem to be easier to dominate at that time.

Speaking of large sites, learning to conserve bids until the right time is very important. Competitive auctions can last for hours, so make sure you have the appropriate time blocked out for your bidding activities. When you see the auction competition waning (down to two or three bidders), that's a smart time to engage.

BID INTELLIGENTLY

How you use your bids is critical to ongoing success as well.

Avoid playing on sites that devalue bids. If you've registered on a website and keep getting emails about their latest bid promotion, you'll be competing with users that have a stockpile of cheap bids and little to lose.

Think of it like the Federal Reserve printing more money; each dollar is worth less.

Early in Josh's bidding experiences, he registered on a site not offering any introductory bid package deals. He bought a 100 package for $75, or 75 cents each.

The next day, he received an email offering a promotional deal. Two days later, the same thing, and they kept coming. He hadn't even placed one 75-cent bid before he realized many competitors would be playing with bids that they only paid 35 cents for.

To make matters worse, this particular site didn't offer refunds for unused bids – another reason why experienced bidders always look over the Terms & Conditions section.

His initial penny auction success made him overconfident and he ended up using $75 worth of bids to win a $10 item.

It is important to bid intelligently. To stay ahead of the game, review a site's policies first for rules that can be detrimental. Pay close attention to win limit restrictions, as well as refund, shipping, and return policies. These vary from site to site.

You also need to consider whether bidding on bids is a good idea. On certain sites, voucher auctions may be very easy to win. Winning 50 bids in exchange for placing five is an excellent return on investment.

However, some penny auctions have very active voucher auctions, creating a bid inflation effect. Throwing your bids into these pots may be a complete waste of time.

 COMMON CENTS

Bid Inflation

We all understand inflation, especially when we go to buy a box of Corn Flakes. Bids you buy for a certain price have a face value. If a particular site gives discounts sparingly, the value of your paid-for bids closely approximate the value of bids used by other players. If you're on a site where discounted bids are the norm, you better get some or you'll be on the wrong side of bid inflation, with bids that are comparatively more expensive in your arsenal.

Bottom line: The goal of any penny auction site is to generate revenue. It's their job to figure out how to do that. Your goal, as a bidder, is to score excellent deals. It's your job to figure that out.

Some sites now offer bonus prizes, such as placing a bid at 15 cents and getting 10 bonus bids. Others offer a community payback option where you get to split profit with the site owners based on the number of bids you place, similar to credit card reward points.

Look over each site's features to determine whether or not they add value or make it harder to win. When you find a site that has what you're looking for and gives you the most bang for your bid package buck, keep playing there.

 COMMON CENTS

Experience-Based Auctions
Winning at penny auctions isn't as easy as it may seem at first. Some auctions, including QuiBids, segregate participation in some auctions, meaning you won't encounter BidDestroyer876 when you try to land that first gift card. He's there, but he's not out of his cage yet. According to its Terms & Conditions section, they do so to "enhance user experience and maintain a viable business model." Translated: If you get crushed like a bug on Day 1, you probably won't be back. This is not a bad thing, but you need to know what you're facing and how the landscape may change.

TARGET THE BEST DEALS

One of the ways to stay ahead of the game is to play smarter than your competition.

Looking to replace your old dusty desktop computer? Chances are you're not the only one.

Hoping to bring home a shiny new iPad? Again, you're one of many.

Learning to target the best deals is almost as important as bidding on the right sites.

To win a new computer or iPad outright is difficult. The competition for popular items is stiff. Powerbidders often go for these items head on, relying on their bidding reputation to carry them through.

But bidding directly on the item you want isn't the only option to victory. One tactic is to bid on less desirable auctions and leverage your wins.

For example, focusing on gift cards with regional limitations (e.g. - Sheetz, Cracker Barrel) can lessen your potential competition and open the way to an easier catch. You can also get deals on cards with a specialized focus, such as Pottery Barn and Ikea.

You can apply the same principles to physical items. Watch auctions and see which go for less consistently. This will blaze a path to easier wins.

It won't be tough to sell your wins with the many local and online venues for classified ads. Many unwanted gift cards can be resold or traded for gift cards that would be more useful to you. We'll discuss in Chapter 8 two companies that will purchase your cards and send you cash or different gift cards in return.

In other words, you can target a lower-demand Pottery Barn card with the intention of swapping it for a higher-demand Starbucks card later on.

Better yet, you can trade in a handful of gift card wins for an Amazon card and then purchase that iPad without the fierce competition most iPad auctions usually bring.

If that seems like too much effort, find a penny auction that offers a swap feature and target the less desirable offerings. There, any gift card or item up for auction can ultimately be exchanged for something else at no extra cost. See the FAQ section of a website or contact the auction owner to see if they offer a swapping option.

Remember what we emphasized in the previous section: Participate on sites giving you the most opportunities to win. After that, your job is to find the deals others are missing and avoid the sharks.

KNOW YOUR OPPONENTS

Speaking of sharks, remember penny auctions are a game of sorts. The goal is to win, and the winner reaps the financial benefits of their success.

If you know more about your opponents than they know about themselves, you put yourself in a position to win more often, save more money, and avoid common mistakes.

In Josh's early penny auction days, he kept track of his opponents' bidding habits manually – sort of like what we asked you to do in Chapter 5.

There are limitations to that approach. It's hard to sit in front of the computer all day. This means you inevitably work with flawed or incomplete data, and to some extent you can only make guesses about your opponents and their bidding habits.

But times have changed.

Coming from a poker background, Mark Streich discovered penny auctions and was immediately fascinated by the question of whether or not penny auctions could be "beat." He understood users could get lucky and win on a fluke, but the bigger question was whether or not bidders could take a strategic approach and win more often.

With some programming knowledge at his fingertips, Streich began to collect raw data to figure out which sites returned the greatest value to bidders and which bidders were most profitable.

"Once I had the data, I realized there was nothing else quite like it," Streich said. "I decided to create a website to share my work with the community."

AllPennyAuctions.com was born.

AllPennyAuctions.com (sometimes abbreviated APA), uses Streich's custom-built software to watch and datamine penny auction websites. Fueled in part by advertising revenue, every bid and every auction is monitored, something no person is capable of tracking alone.

"After the data is collected, we have dozens of manual validation processes, and anomaly analysis reports that are checked daily," he said. "We also make the raw data used in our reporting available back to site owners themselves. This (data) can be compared with their own internal numbers to verify our accuracy."

APA's tracking isn't perfect. Streich is shooting for the most accurate numbers possible. When users find inaccuracies or missing data and pass that along, the discoveries can result in a review of the software coding and corrections to historical data.

In other words, the data keep getting better and better.

The user name search is the site's most popular feature. It's an easy way to determine if the user that just outbid you is willing to put hundreds of bids into an item or is just a jumper hoping for a cheap win. It's also a great way to analyze the strategies of top bidders and see how they make money in penny auctions.

As penny auctions grow in popularity, we expect to see more sites like AllPennyAuctions.com. Your own research combined with a healthy dose of AllPennyAuctions.com will help you avoid the sharks and stay ahead of the game.

SPOT RED FLAGS

As we said earlier, you should keep playing at sites where you win regularly. At the same time, you should continue to examine new possibilities.

When searching for new auctions, watch for red flags. Even experienced bidders have been duped by dishonest sites.

 COMMON CENTS

Red Flags

If you're a NASCAR fan, you know a red flag stops the race. But the use of red flag as a warning symbol goes back earlier than Richard Petty and Fireball Roberts. The Oxford English Dictionary used the term in the 1600s, relating it to military battles. Of course, red means stop, as in lights, signs, and trains. Red flags also let lifeguards tell you where not to swim. And with penny auctions, red flags should tell you to look elsewhere.

The first flag is a lack of contact information. If a site hides contacts, be concerned. Look for a physical address, phone number, and email for starters. If that information isn't present, the site may have something to hide and you should avoid playing there.

Demand transparency and don't spend your money in dark alleys.

Second, if you find a new site auctioning a car, four MacBooks, ten TVs, and a $1,000 pinball machine – all in the same week – have some doubts.

You can check website traffic information through a service like Alexa.com or Compete.com. These won't give you a perfect traffic measurement, but they will gauge how many unique visitors a site generates each day. If a site is averaging less than 1,000 unique visits a month, it doesn't have the traffic to be auctioning big ticket items.

Traffic information will also help you spot another flag: Strange bidding behaviors. If you notice bidding that seems completely illogical on a site that appears to have very little traffic – such as bidders furiously battling for a $10 gift card and competing into the $5 range – stay away.

Bidders can sometimes compete illogically. But heavy competition on a relatively young site may mean the owner is using bot bidders to artificially inflate prices. Though there isn't a simple way to identify bot bidding – most bots are programmed to bid randomly up to a certain price – trust your gut instinct and only bid at places that inspire confidence.

As you get acclimated to the penny auction community, you will begin to recognize certain user names. If you don't see any of those names on a site you're considering, you've spotted another flag. Search for reviews or move on to a different site.

Some bidders think they can stay ahead of the game by signing up on new websites and winning items before everybody else arrives. Though we understand the logic, you run a greater risk in participating on a site with no track record.

PENNY WISE

8

NICKELS & DIMES

*"You have to grab moments when they happen.
I like to improvise and ad lib."*
—Actor Denzel Washington

Winning penny auctions is great, but what's next?

Since most readers of this book are like us and have a limited budget, we'd like to offer a few suggestions for turning your penny auction wins into real profit.

After all, you want to be sure this newfound hobby is sustainable.

Quick aside: If you aren't operating on a limited budget, you don't need this chapter. Before skipping to Chapter 8, feel free to invest some of your limitless funds into purchasing a few extra copies of this book. We won't mind.

RESELLING YOUR ITEMS

Once you learn to play the game successfully, you can win items at less than retail on a regular basis.

This is great way to get Christmas shopping done early and less expensively. You can also knock items off your own needs list and spend less.

Another option is to monetize your wins by selling items for more than what you paid. This isn't something we've done much, but it is a sound option pursued by some successful buyers.

Before going any further, it's important to note a couple of things.

First, some penny auction websites prohibit resellers from bidding in their auctions. Read the Terms & Conditions of each site before attempting to resell your items.

Just like elementary school, someone will tell on you if they discover you are reselling your wins when you shouldn't be. Failure to follow Terms & Conditions may lead to your account being banned.

If a site gives you freedom to flip with your wins, you have plenty of online and local options for that. We'll highlight a few and leave the rest to your entrepreneurial and exploratory spirit.

 COMMON CENTS

Flip

Most commonly associated with real estate, flipping is buying something at a bargain with the intention of turning it around – or flipping it – quickly for a profit. Pulling this off depends on the relative demand of the item and your success at truly getting stuff for pennies on the dollar. Buying toy wristwatches for a few bucks over retail, for example, won't really do it for you. Consistently landing certain kinds of in-demand merchandise at a low price might. Be careful, though, making this happen in practice is not very easy.

Second, and this is a big one: Remember the tax man. We're not going to dispense tax advice; it's not our area. It is important to note the Internal Revenue Service and various states have guidelines on what's taxable and what's not, and what's a hobby and what's not.

If you're doing this regularly and with the intention to make money, it's likely any net income is taxable in some form. You should keep records of your transactions. Your losses and related costs of buying, for example, can offset your profits.

Bottom line: If you get really good at this, and we hope you do, keep records and do a little research into the tax implications of your own situation.

USING EBAY

In spite of the deep discounts that penny auctions have to offer, some consumers still believe eBay is the best place to get a deal.

That leaves you two options.

You could try to help them understand how penny auctions work or cash in on their allegiance to the kingdom of eBay.

We'll leave that decision up to you.

If you decide to resell on eBay, you have the distinct advantage of low-balling virtually everybody else, since you can fetch items at a much better price than most eBay vendors.

To sell successfully through eBay, list the items with the greatest demand (electronics tend to be high on the list) and sell items in lower demand elsewhere.

You shouldn't have problems selling your items if you take good pictures and set the price appropriately. Bidders on eBay are happy to purchase an item at 10 to 20 percent off retail, and both parties win if you originally purchased the item for half off the retail price.

The disadvantages of selling on eBay are seller fees and shipping responsibilities.

Amazon.com also allows you to post and sell items, giving you another large marketplace for monetizing wins.

CRAIGSLIST AND LOCAL CLASSIFIEDS

If you prefer to sell your items locally, avoiding the eBay seller fees and shipping hassle, Craigslist is a good way to go. Buyers seem to expect greater discounts here, so be prepared to haggle and negotiate.

Craigslist is a better site for selling niche items. It doesn't cost you anything to list your wins and the buyers come to you.

The site is mostly centered around metropolitan areas. So if you live in the back country, you may need to investigate other classified websites in your neck of the woods.

Many local newspapers offer free or inexpensive print and online classifieds, so don't be afraid to experiment with different options to reach as many local buyers as possible.

 COMMON CENTS

Classifieds

Small ads in boxes were long a mainstay of daily newspapers, joining automobile dealers, Realtors, and department stores in fueling print products' bottom line. The term classifieds comes from the headings ads were grouped under, from "Used Chryslers" to "Help Wanted - Penny Auction Pros." Newspapers have put such ads online and the category has a range of new competition, but the term has stuck.

FACEBOOK

In case you didn't realize it, or don't go to the movies, Facebook is here to stay.

While your personal privacy may be lost and gone forever, the opportunities to monetize your winnings clearly reside in social networks.

As long as you have a few online friends, that is.

Buy.com currently offers a Facebook plug-in called Garage Sale. This service, currently in testing, allows you to post items for sale directly on your profile page.

Take advantage of all those profile stalkers and sell your goods with little effort.

Buy.com takes a 5 percent commission for every sale you make, but they also guarantee secure transactions and easy payouts by check or PayPal. See buy.com/garagesale for more information.

Oodle.com, a Craigslist competitor, is also harnessing the power of Facebook in an attempt to reinvent online classifieds. Their app, Marketplace on Facebook, offers similar opportunities to Garage Sale. See apps.facebook.com for more information.

Facebook offers convenient opportunities for selling your wins, but you may need to stop ignoring all of those friend requests.

RESELLING GIFT CARDS

Consumers are most comfortable buying items they can touch, see, or feel. Electronics, housewares, and other tangible items are easy to sell if the price is right.

Selling gift cards is a different story.

Gift cards hold an invisible value, and trying to peddle these electronic cards may be met with some suspicion.

It makes sense. Potential buyers have to trust the invisible value you claim the card has is the actual value of the card. There are number of ways you can verify this, but the hassle probably isn't worth your time.

Buyers may also wonder why someone would be willing to sell a $25 gift card for $15. Discount the card too much and they'll think it's stolen. Discount too little and you won't get their attention.

Insert your own doubts here.

Thankfully, there are several reputable vendors that purchase unused and partially-used gift cards.

PlasticJungle.com will pay up to 92 percent of the verified balance of your unwanted gift cards. You can request payouts via check, PayPal, or Amazon credit. The process is very simple. The only catch is gift cards must have a balance of $25 or more.

CardPool.com is another vendor offering the service, with the aforementioned promise of up to 92 percent cash back for gift cards you're willing to sell.

Reviews for both services are stellar, and consumers feel more confident buying gift cards here than they would through your eBay alter-ego.

 **PENNY POINTS**

Start Your Own Online Store
If you're ready to cut out the middleman, you may want to consider opening your own online marketplace. Starting an e-commerce website may seem like a lofty task. Back in the late '90s, it was. But a new day has arrived. A variety of websites give you the flexibility of opening your own, professional e-commerce website in a matter of minutes.

1. Find a place. Sites such as Shopify.com, HighWire.com, and BigCartel.com offer flexible plans and pricing.

2. Get to work. You can post items, track inventory, analyze visitor statistics, and process orders securely for as little as $9.99 per month.

3. Read the fine print. Avoid hidden fees and long term contracts.

4. Don't forget the tax man. While buyers may not find your site, the IRS probably will.

TRADING AND BARTERING

Once you've filled your vacation jar with nickels and dimes (i.e. - real money), you may start thinking of other creative ways to monetize.

A few thousand years ago, most human beings were nomads. That is, they wandered from place to place in search of food and other valuable commodities. As these small roaming clans learned how to farm, they finally gave up on their mobile way of life and settled down. This marked the establishment of stable communities (Note to those with some history background: We're using the word "stable" loosely).

At that time, there was no monetary system. Most business transactions were conducted by bartering with your neighbors to get what was needed.

Person Y offers Person X two pigs in exchange for a really awesome cow. If the terms are agreeable to both parties, they shake hands and make the switch.

You can do the same thing with your penny auction wins.

TheBidLounge.com and TheBiddersNetwork.com both offer areas for bidders to trade, swap and barter. Find the right person and make a deal.

 COMMON CENTS

Invites
Tell a friend and make a buck. Or at least a bid. Like pretty much any business, penny auctions will pay you for referrals. In this case, it's not cash you get but, what else, bids. When you invite someone to become a player and register on a penny auction site, the owners will often give you free bids as a bonus. This is not a bad thing, provided your friend is someone who won't hold it against you that they lost $60 worth of bids and all they got was a lousy t-shirt you gave them at the beach. If you're worried about your friendship, don't invite.

DONATING TO CHARITY

You may have encountered a few wisdom sayings pertaining to power or success and the corrupting effects they can have on the human frame. As you become a bidding king or queen, avoid morphing into a bidding despot.

Though bidding success in no way obligates you to help anyone else, it should inevitably lead you to do so.

Monetizing your wins is a great move for your personal books. (See the IRS notes.) Donating your wins is a great move for your personal well-being and the well-being of those around you, too.

We'd like to leave you with a clarion call to think seriously about the people and opportunities that exist in your local community. Penny auctions give you an opportunity to be more generous than ever before. Develop a healthy blend of being profitable and charitable.

Show those CEOs how it's done.

9

STARTING YOUR OWN WEBSITE

*"We cannot do everything at once,
but we can do something at once."*
—Former U.S. President Calvin Coolidge

By now, you may be hatching plans for your own penny auction website. Or you might be wondering if it's too late to get in the game.

With annual revenues pegged above $500 million, such a desire is understandable.

A word of advice: Proceed with caution.

Remember Swoopo, the pioneer of online penny auctions. Even with major backing from venture capital firms, it was unable to sustain the business needed to survive.

This book doesn't tell the story of Wavee or BigDeal, two other large sites that closed their doors for good. Both were popular during their heyday. The latter was taken over by another site; the former shut down in part due to a settlement with regulators in Georgia, who also required the site to pay hundreds of thousands of dollars in penalties.

As you can imagine, the list of closed sites can and will go on. Some operators will approach and cross ethical lines. They should – and some will – go out of business.

Still, there is money to be made. If you're focused on getting a share of it, we'll offer up some realistic expectations and remind you that going the distance requires more than just a few dollars and some energy drinks.

WHERE TO START

The first thing to recognize is you are getting your foot in the door a bit late. The industry is changing rapidly, leaving little room for a poorly planned, poorly executed penny auction venture.

But there are signs of growth and development. Making a successful entry into the world of penny auctions isn't out of the question – if you've done your homework.

Case in point: Bid-Bob.com.

Launched in May 2011, Bid-Bob's success is palpable and seems to be a demonstration it's not too late to make a successful run.

Bob MacReynolds, president of Bid-Bob.com, credits a solid business plan as one of the primary reasons for its positive growth to date.

"As in any business, you need a business plan with a clear objective of why you are entering the market and how you plan to differentiate from the competition," he said. "I have seen many sites that open and try to differentiate themselves with claims like 'the most honest auction site' or we'll have 'the best customer service' in the industry.'"

Such claims don't guarantee success, he said.

Honesty and customer service should be a part of your initial business plan (and your character for that matter), but a successful plan doesn't stop there. Your business plan must include unique ingredients other sites are lacking.

You also need to spend time doing "due diligence," a standard business and legal practice encompassing an investigation into all the facts, finances, and realities of your proposed business, including your ability to pull it off. After your research, you should have a complete understanding of the risks in front of you.

SITE DESIGN AND PROGRAMMING

Once you've built a rock-solid business plan, you need to think about the infrastructure needed to power your website.

Should you purchase a penny auction script or hire a custom developer? What about hosting? Should you conduct usability testing?

Such questions highlight a few of the crucial pre-launch choices.

 COMMON CENTS

Package

Unless you're Bill Gates, and even if you are, we doubt you'll want to sit down and write a script for your very own penny auction site. If you're of a mind to start one, you'll be shopping for a software package. Packages can include hosting of your site and are designed for various levels of complexity, depending on the number of simultaneous bidders you expect will be using your site. Packages can also have plug-ins, similar to what you'd find on a WordPress platform for your very own blog, and prices depend on how many pennies you want to spend.

One site, phpPennyAuction.com, offers a turn-key penny auction script for less than $1,000. This is a functional penny auction "engine" you can use the power your site, eliminating the need to start from ground zero.

The standard package from phpPennyAuction currently includes nine different auction types, multiple payment gateways, integration with social networks, and two months of free support. The package also includes script installation on the customer's server of choice.

But is it enough?

Before moving forward with any script purchase, contact penny auction owners who are using the script. The About Us or Contact page should provide you with sufficient information to get in touch. Many owners are willing to help.

Ask about unexpected costs, advantages, and disadvantages before committing to any pre-packaged solution.

Based on your particular plan, a pre-packaged script may not do all you need. It may lack the unique features you hope to integrate or the personalized touch of an experienced web developer.

Custom development can be costly – in the range of $5,000 and up – but it may be what you need.

Among those who followed this route is Rob Ashe, founder of Moloyo.com. He envisioned a site where users could sell their own items. From a business standpoint, this model eliminates much of the merchandise overhead. Users supply the items for each auction and he generates a small commission for each sale through the site.

(Ashe is also part of TheBiddersNetwork.com with co-author Josh Waldron, a bidder-driven, first-stop site with reviews, deals, forums, and auctions.)

Moloyo required months of programming. The finished product allows users to post items, set reserves, split profits, and interact via a variety of social networking features.

After researching some of the script options, Bob MacReynolds and his business partners decided custom development was a necessity for them, too.

Unique web features were a strategic element of the Bid-Bob business plan, and a successful deployment of those features necessitated the services of a reliable development company.

"Small issues like changing your win limits, refunding bidpack purchases, trouble-shooting bidding problems . . . can become big problems if you don't have a development company backing you up," MacReynolds said.

Then there's hosting. Penny auction websites are server-intensive. If you have children, take a brief moment to remind yourself of what it's like to have all of them trying to communicate something to you at once.

Utter chaos.

Translate this to penny auctions. Multiple, simultaneous, timed auctions, and bidders spread throughout the country, often bidding within milliseconds of each other. A basic hosting package won't be able to handle the demands of a very active penny auction website.

Countless sites market themselves well to bidders pre-launch only to lose the luster with a disastrous, nail-in-the-coffin launch day.

Faulty timers, voided auctions, and a crashed website will kill any momentum you've built for your site, so test extensively and take the necessary precautions in pursuit of a reliable hosting option.

If the details seem overwhelming, penny auction forums such as PennyBurners.com and PennyAuctionHelp.com offer places for current and prospective auction owners to ask tough questions and get answers.

Throughout the design and development process, adopt the mantra "cheap isn't always better." Look at sites doing it well and you'll notice common theme: A functional, reliable, and well-designed website.

Remind yourself that every decision you make is a crucial step on the path to success, even if such success isn't guaranteed.

 COMMON CENTS

Gateway

A payment gateway is the conduit used to process payments from credit card companies and customer checking accounts directly to your bank account. Some examples are LinkPoint, Authorize.net, Paypal and Google Checkout. (That's right. Google IS into everything.) These vendors handle literally billions of dollars of transactions, so they can certainly take on your penny auction site. In choosing a route to go, consider how they handle fees, fraud, setup, and maintenance. Find the size that fits your site and your aspirations.

GETTING THE MERCHANDISE

As a new penny auction, you'll need to decide where to buy items you plan to auction. Obviously, the goal is to get the best deal possible on your merchandise while offering bidders items they want.

Competitive prices and reliable shipping make Amazon.com a site many owners turn to regularly. Buying all kinds of merchandise through Amazon also eliminates the overhead of maintaining a warehouse and shipping items manually.

But don't stop with Amazon, and don't be afraid to think outside the box. Look to maximize profit on every auction and constantly re-evaluate your options.

Also, take advantage of Internet bargain websites. They're everywhere, and they're competing with each other. (Side note: If you didn't know that, you might want to re-consider starting a penny auction website.)

Browse these sites daily. When you see a closeout or drastic sale, it may be worth your time to scoop up large quantities of this stuff for future auctions. You can turn your wife's scrapbooking room or your husband's garage into a mini-warehouse if you have profitability to show for it – and their permission, of course.

If you want to gain an edge on your competitors, keep your product offerings fresh and unique. Some sites even poll customers to see what items they would be willing to bid on.

If your site grows large enough, new discounted merchandise opportunities may be available to you. Wholesale and drop shipping companies will offer extensive discounts to websites that conduct the right number of transactions.

Just ask QuiBids or SkoreIt!.

STAYING IN BUSINESS

Neither of us can speak from an owner's perspective, but we can tell you from various interactions there are plenty of colorful personalities to go around.

The bidding community is diverse.

When you launch your site, make sure you have clear, enforceable Terms & Conditions section. Encourage bidders to familiarize themselves with the guidelines and seek to create an environment the greatest number of users can appreciate.

Again, this is a key element of Bid-Bob.com.

"We make decisions based on the best interests of the user base as a whole," said MacReynolds, who adds the importance of taking each customer seriously doesn't mean you are "going to make everyone happy."

Plan to dedicate a significant portion of your time to responding to customer emails and make necessary changes based on consistent user feedback.

Once you launch your well-planned, technologically prepared, merchandise-driven, bidder-centric website, you still have the future to consider.

 COMMON CENTS

SMS

Bids come in all shapes and sizes. A common way to enable as many as possible to land on your site is SMS. Short Message Service is a text-messaging feature of various communications devices. Some penny auction packages allow customers to bid via SMS. To enable this, your software needs to be set up to handle this. You should also include what's called "reverse SMS billing" so the message sender is not the one charged for the cost of the message received. If you're at this point, you're getting pretty involved and need to get professional help – for the technology side, that is.

When the honeymoon period is over, bidders will look for sites offering them the best bidding experience and value. It's simple economics.

Customer retention is the biggest issue you will face post-launch. This is where experience as a bidder and a member of the penny auction community is genuinely valuable.

In examining the rise and fall of 100+ sites, essential elements for continued, successful operations emerge. These elements won't guarantee survival, but if you're lacking any of the four, we can tell you the missing piece will likely lead to your eventual downfall.

>> Stay Committed to Customer Service and Transparency >>

Like it or not, bidders will network beyond the walls of your website. Negative feedback spreads quickly. But most bidders are happy to recommend sites they believe "do things the right way."

If you drop the ball on customer service, it will take you twice the effort to re-establish your reputation. We could repeat the rule of treating others like you want to be treated. You can't go wrong there.

Like it or not, bidders will network beyond the walls of your website. Negative feedback spreads quickly. But most bidders are happy to recommend sites they believe "do things the right way."

If you drop the ball on customer service, it will take you twice the effort to re-establish your reputation.

>> Host Worthwhile Contests and Promotions >>

Contests give users a reason to re-engage with your site. Make sure the contests you host benefit both the site and the bidder. Don't over complicate the contest requirements. Rather, give users a reason to connect with your site continually.

Sites sometimes host contests for the best video testimonials or the most customer referrals. We've even spotted a contest for the biggest loser, though we're not sure you want to be that guy.

Promotions encourage users to buy bids on your site instead of somewhere else. Plan promotions carefully, as undervaluing bids can create another set of issues.

Look to effectively integrate contests and promotions with Facebook, as this network has internal and external marketing benefits.

>> Add New Features & Make Adjustments Where Necessary >>
Avoid stagnancy. As the penny auction model continues to evolve, bidders roam around looking for websites offering the best value and the most enjoyable bidding experience.

Remember our earlier discussion of FarmVille?

Some sites offer auctions based on user experience level, such as beginner, intermediate, or expert. Others offer profit-sharing opportunities (e.g. – the last three unique bidders in an auction split the "pot") or progressive-type auctions (e.g. – the higher the final bid, the higher the value of the item you win). Increasingly, as we mentioned, sites are integrating creative games to keep things interesting.

None of these variations existed when we first started experimenting with penny auctions, so these changes demonstrate that creativity and flexibility will determine future growth.

As an owner, never get comfortable with what you have to offer and be sure to provide the best value to as many of your bidders as possible.

>> Keep Marketing Your Website >>
Owners will tell you revenue can fluctuate, sometimes sharply.

When you have a good month, don't fill your swimming pool with all of that cash. Reinvest in advertising opportunities and other marketing aspects.

Many penny auction information websites and forums offer advertising opportunities. But advertising on sites like PennyAuctionList.com has its limitations. In essence, you're advertising to people who may already be familiar with penny auctions.

Start there, but think bigger.

Google AdWords, local newspaper and television venues, radio spots, airplanes with banners, well-trained carrier pigeons. The possibilities are virtually endless.

Make it a goal to continue building the user base. Then, when some bidders inevitably wander away, you have new customers to impress.

Again, follow some simple rules.

Plan. Execute. Grow. Adapt. Grow Again.

If you can follow that framework, you may just have what it takes to run your own site successfully.

 **PENNY POINTS**

Killer Customer Service
Here are some simple rules to follow in meeting the first of the four tests:

1. Communicate with bidders. Don't keep rules, changes, and guidelines hidden. Be clear.

2. Ship your items quickly. Get them out the door and delivered. Word of your follow-through will spread.

3. Go the extra mile. Any extra steps, even costly ones, are likely to return levels of loyalty and respect worth your time and trouble.

4. Admit your mistakes. If you've learned anything from any number of fill-in-the-blank scandals, this is the first lesson.

5. Avoid questionable or fraudulent activities. Make a wrong step here and you may never be able to fully recover.

10

THE PIGGYBANK

"Arriving at one goal is the starting point to another"
—American philosopher John Dewey

We hope this book has given you a greater understanding of the world of penny auctions – both the possibilities and the pitfalls.

There is no shortage of sites. New ones are starting and some are shutting down. Below is a brief introduction to several that currently meet the criteria of the Penny Auction List directory.

These are sites that have a phone, physical address, and/or email. They also offer easily accessible terms of use that pledge to prohibit shady practices and testimonials or user confirmation of their quality. Other sites not listed may very well meet the same standard.

This chapter also includes other places to go for deals and information, as well as some of the sources we used in writing this book.

The information is current as of the time of publication and is not exclusive of what a site offers or a guarantee such benefits are still available. Features and promotions are subject to change.

One other note: Listing here does not imply our endorsement. We can't vouch for the safety or fairness of a particular site. We encourage you to research and apply the lessons of this book in finding a place to buy online.

AUCTION SITES

7thBid.com
Features: Reserve auctions, every seventh bid is free, every seventh bundle is free.
Promotions: Three free bids at signup.

Beezid.com
Features: Beginner auctions, early bird auctions, large product selection.
Promotions: Ten free bids at signup.

Bid-Bob.com
Features: Beginner auctions, charitable giving program, bonus prizes.
Promotions: Contact Bid-Bob for current promotions.

BidCactus.com
Features: Wide range of items, focus on customer support.
Promotions: Use code K2T8BC to get $10 off your first auction win.

BidPigs.com
Features: Reward points, beginner auctions, free bid Fridays, bid-to-buy option on some auctions.
Promotions: Three free bids at signup.

Bids4Cheap.com
Features: Multiple auction formats, 30-cent bids.
Promotions: 20% bonus bids with first bid package purchase.

Dibzees.com
Features: 50-cent bids, beginner auctions, swap-it feature
Promotions: Contact Dibzees for current promotions.

Moloyo.com

Features: Users can set reserve prices and sell items, combines site with social networks.

Promotions: Contact Moloyo for current promotions.

Nailbidder.com

Features: Free UPS ground shipping on all auctions.

Promotions: Five free bids at signup.

PennyPrizes.com

Features: Beginner, mystery, and progressive auctions, easy-to-enter bid promos.

Promotions: 10 free bids at signup.

PennyPurses.com

Features: Rookie and sudden-death auctions, future bid feature.

Promotions: Free shipping on all auctions.

PulseAuction.com

Features: Auction "unlock keys" which allow unlimited bidding in exchange for a small entry fee.

Promotions: $1 unlock key at signup.

QuiBids.com

Features: Buy-it-now feature on every auction, QuiBids 101 tips area, large product selection.

Promotions: Bonus bids for signup, referrals, and more.

SellMoo.com

Features: Buy-it-now and live customer service features, reward points, bidder forum.

Promotions: Three free bids at signup.

ShareTheSpoils.com

Features: Every auction lets the last three unique bidders split half the pot.

Promotions: Two free bids at signup.

SkoreIt.com
Features: Automatic bidding service, buy it now feature on select auctions, large product selection.
Promotions: Use "BIDNOW" for $10 of free bids.

TheSmartBid.com
Features: Lowest unique bid auction format.
Promotions: $3 credit at signup.

REVIEWS, FORUMS, DISCOUNTS, AND MORE

You're not alone in the world of penny auctions. Several locations offer forums to swap information and details. Some may suit your style; some won't. Details are not always verified, either, so consider the source as you evaluate.

Other sites serve as a clearinghouse of news, reviews, statistics, and discounts. Some are owned or controlled by principals or former owners of penny auction sites. We've noted some such relationships below.

Pennywisethebook.com
Useful tools for bidders and links to resources.

AllPennyAuctions.com
Offers a detailed analysis of many penny auction sites and tracks the bidding habits of possible opponents.

CheapBidpacks.com
Lists promo codes for various penny auction sites. Users and owners can upload promo codes of their own. Operated by co-author Josh Waldron.

PennyAuctionCoupon.com
The first Groupon-style coupon site. Offers a daily deal for small bidpacks, usually in the range of 50-75 percent off. Operated by David Asselin of pennyauction.ca.

PennyAuctionHelp.com
Includes forums sponsored by penny auction sites and offers bid promotions. Operated by Jeremy Hetrick of BidPigs.com.

PennyAuctionList.com
A carefully filtered directory of penny auctions. Includes news, reviews, and promo codes. Site owned by co-author Josh Waldron.

PennyAuctionPromo.com
Offers 2 for 1 type deals. Operated by David Asselin of pennyauction.ca.

PennyAuctionScore.com
Hosts a large selection of penny auction reviews. Operated by David Asselin of pennyauction.ca.

PennyAuctionWatch.com
The first penny auction forum to hit the internet. Site has news, promotions, and discussion threads.

PennyBurners.com
Verifies authenticity of various penny auctions. Site also integrates with Penny Talk Radio, a weekly penny auction podcast.

TheBidLounge.com
One of the most active penny auction forums on the web. Lots of ads. Integrates social networking features.

TheBiddersNetwork.com
Designed to be a gateway, first-stop site to access reviews, deals, forums, and auctions. Owned by co-author Josh Waldron and Moloyo.com principal Rob Ashe.

SOURCES FOR PENNY WISE

We talked with dozens of penny auction operators, players, industry followers, and more. Each provided important insights and details.

Along with personal interviews and examination of many auction sites, we used a range of other resources, including the following:

-Alexander, Kristen. "Some Penny Auctions Use Cheap Tricks to Cheat Consumers." Washington State Office of the Attorney General's *All Consuming Blog*, 28 September 2010.

-Augenblick, Ned. "Consumer and Producer Behavior in the Market for Penny Auctions: A Theoretical and Empirical Analysis." Mimeo, Stanford University, 28 December 2009.

-"Be Cautious of Penny Auction Sites." *Better Business Bureau News Center*, 1 October 2010.

-Byers, John, Michael Mitzenmacher, and Georgios Zervas. "Information Asymmetries in Pay-Per-Bid Auctions: How Swoopo Makes Bank." *Electronic Commerce: Proceedings of the 11th ACM Conference on Electronic Commerce*, 5 January 2010.

-Cohen, Deborah. "Entrepreneur Turns Pennies into Million-Dollar Business." *Reuters*, 9 June 2010.

-Dubois, Shelley. "Penny Auctions Bet on Chump Change." *Wired*, 21-22 January 2010.

-Grigoriadis, Vanessa. "Ol' Mark Pincus Had a Farm ...." *Vanity Fair*, June 2011.

-Kim, Susanna. "Regulators Move on Penny Auction Sites After Complaints." *ABC News*, 19 August 2011.

-Locke, Lawrence A. vs. QuiBids LLC. Class Action Case No. 5:10-cv-01277-W. *United States District Court for the Western District of Oklahoma,* 8 December 2010.

-Luscombe, Belinda. "Losing Your Cents." *Time,* 17 June 2010.

-"Online Penny Auctions: Nothing for Something?" *Federal Trade Commission Consumer Alert,* August 2011.

-Pennells, Sarah. "Penny Web Auctions Under Scrutiny." *BBC News,* 20 December 2008.

-Penny Auction Solutions Inc. Form S-1. *United States Security and Exchange Commission,* 3 February 2011.

-Platt, Brennan, Joseph Price, and Henry Tappen. "Pay-to-Bid Auctions." Mimeo, Brigham Young University, 22 September 2010.

-Stone, Brad. "Penny Auction Sites Hurt by Glut of Competitors." *Bloomberg Businessweek,* 12 August 2010.

-Stone, Brad. "Sites Ask Users to Spend to Save." *The New York Times,* 17 August 2009.

-Sullivan, Bob. "An iPad for $2.82, or Illegal Gambling?" *The Red Tape Chronicles* on msnbc.com, 18 February 2011.

-"The Heyday of the Auction." *The Economist,* 22 July 1999.

-Vaknin, Sam. "Europe and the Spectrum of Auctions." *Global Politician,* 17 January 2006.

-Walker, Tom. "Founders of Oklahoma City-based QuiBids Earn an A in Entrepreneurship, Job Creation." *The Oklahoman,* 7 June 2011.

-Wingfield, Nick. "Virtual Products, Real Profits: Players Spend on Zynga's Games, but Quality Turns Some Off." *The Wall Street Journal*, 9 September 2011.

-Zimmerman, Ann. "Penny Auctions Draw Bidders With Bargains, Suspense." *The Wall Street Journal*, 17 August 2011.

ABOUT THE AUTHORS

Ken Knelly spent a dozen years as a print journalist, earning regional and national recognition. He owns Clearberries, a strategic communications firm specializing in writing, editing, and crafting messages for businesses and nonprofits, and works for a small college. He lives in Northeastern Pennsylvania with his wife and three children.

Website: clearberries.com

Josh Waldron is the creator and owner of PennyAuctionList.com, a dynamic one-stop, user-oriented site featuring news, ratings, and more. He also owns Studio JWAL, an award-winning web-design firm, and is a high school social studies teacher. He lives in the scenic Blue Ridge Mountains of Virginia with his wife and two children.

Website: studiojwal.com